Writing the Critical Essay

Self-Mutilation

An **OPPOSING**  **VIEWPOINTS® Guide**

Lauri S. Friedman, *Book Editor*

**OPPOSING
VIEWPOINTS®
SERIES**

GREENHAVEN PRESS
A part of Gale, Cengage Learning

GALE
CENGAGE Learning

Detroit • New York • San Francisco • New Haven, Conn • Waterville, Maine • London

Christine Nasso, *Publisher*
Elizabeth Des Chenes, *Managing Editor*

© 2009 Greenhaven Press, a part of Gale, Cengage Learning

For more information, contact:
Greenhaven Press
27500 Drake Rd.
Farmington Hills, MI 48331-3535
Or you can visit our Internet site at gale.cengage.com

For product information and technology assistance, contact us at

Gale Customer Support, 1-800-877-4253
For permission to use material from this text or product, submit all requests online at www.cengage.com/permissions

Further permissions questions can be emailed to permissionrequest@cengage.com

Articles in Greenhaven Press anthologies are often edited for length to meet page requirements. In addition, original titles of these works are changed to clearly present the main thesis and to explicitly indicate the author's opinion. Every effort is made to ensure that Greenhaven Press accurately reflects the original intent of the authors. Every effort has been made to trace the owners of copyrighted material.

Cover image Barrett_Forster/Stone/Getty Images.

LIBRARY OF CONGRESS CATALOGING-IN-PUBLICATION DATA

Self-mutilation / Lauri S. Friedman, book editor.
    p. cm. — (Writing the critical essay: an opposing viewpoints guide)
  Includes bibliographical references and index.
  ISBN 978-0-7377-4266-4 (hardcover)
  1. Self-mutilation. 2. Self-mutilation in adolescence. I. Friedman, Lauri S.
  RC552.S4S4572 2009
  616.85'8200835—dc22
 	
                                                            2008033612

Printed in the United States of America
1 2 3 4 5 6 7 12 11 10 09 08

CONTENTS

Examining the state of writing and how it is taught in the United States was the official purpose of the National Commission on Writing in America's Schools and Colleges. The commission, made up of teachers, school administrators, business leaders, and college and university presidents, released its first report in 2003. "Despite the best efforts of many educators," commissioners argued, "writing has not received the full attention it deserves." Among the findings of the commission was that most fourth-grade students spent less than three hours a week writing, that three-quarters of high school seniors never receive a writing assignment in their history or social studies classes, and that more than 50 percent of first-year students in college have problems writing error-free papers. The commission called for a "cultural sea change" that would increase the emphasis on writing for both elementary and secondary schools. These conclusions have made some educators realize that writing must be emphasized in the curriculum. As colleges are demanding an ever-higher level of writing proficiency from incoming students, schools must respond by making students more competent writers. In response to these concerns, the SAT, an influential standardized test used for college admissions, required an essay for the first time in 2005.

Books in the Writing the Critical Essay: An Opposing Viewpoints Guide series use the patented Opposing Viewpoints format to help students learn to organize ideas and arguments and to write essays using common critical writing techniques. Each book in the series focuses on a particular type of essay writing—including expository, persuasive, descriptive, and narrative—that students learn while being taught both the five-paragraph essay as well as longer pieces of writing that have an opinionated focus. These guides include everything necessary to help students research, outline, draft, edit, and ultimately write successful essays across the curriculum, including essays for the SAT.

Using Opposing Viewpoints

This series is inspired by and builds upon Greenhaven Press's acclaimed Opposing Viewpoints series. As in the

Foreword

parent series, each book in the Writing the Critical Essay series focuses on a timely and controversial social issue that provides lots of opportunities for creating thought-provoking essays. The first section of each volume begins with a brief introductory essay that provides context for the opposing viewpoints that follow. These articles are chosen for their accessibility and clearly stated views. The thesis of each article is made explicit in the article's title and is accentuated by its pairing with an opposing or alternative view. These essays are both models of persuasive writing techniques and valuable research material that students can mine to write their own informed essays. Guided reading and discussion questions help lead students to key ideas and writing techniques presented in the selections.

The second section of each book begins with a preface discussing the format of the essays and examining characteristics of the featured essay type. Model five-paragraph and longer essays then demonstrate that essay type. The essays are annotated so that key writing elements and techniques are pointed out to the student. Sequential, step-by-step exercises help students construct and refine thesis statements; organize material into outlines; analyze and try out writing techniques; write transitions, introductions, and conclusions; and incorporate quotations and other researched material. Ultimately, students construct their own compositions using the designated essay type.

The third section of each volume provides additional research material and writing prompts to help the student. Additional facts about the topic of the book serve as a convenient source of supporting material for essays. Other features help students go beyond the book for their research. Like other Greenhaven Press books, each book in the Writing the Critical Essay series includes bibliographic listings of relevant periodical articles, books, Web sites, and organizations to contact.

Writing the Critical Essay: An Opposing Viewpoints Guide will help students master essay techniques that can be used in any discipline.

Self-Mutilation Around the Globe

Self-mutilation—the addictive, destructive tendency of some persons to cope with anxiety, depression, frustration, and severe emotional pain by cutting, scratching, burning, punching, strangling, or otherwise hurting themselves—is a growing problem with international roots. Self-mutilators have been identified in dozens of countries and often share the same emotional triggers for their behavior.

In the United States, it is estimated that nearly 3 million people self-mutilate. As with many trends, in America self-mutilation has become associated with some of the biggest stars in Hollywood: Angelina Jolie, Christina Ricci, Nicole Ritchie, and Courtney Love are just a few of the celebrities who have publicly admitted to cutting or otherwise hurting themselves to dull their emotional pain. Their actions symbolize a growing trend among America's youth: The *New York Times* reports that experts estimate that self-injury is practiced by 15 percent of the general adolescent population, with a whopping 17 percent of college students admitting in anonymous polls that they have practiced some form of self-harm. Self-mutilation has become such a prominent problem in American schools that beginning in 2006, March 1 was declared by public officials to be National Self-Injury Awareness Day.

America's northern neighbor also experiences problems with self-mutilation: Though Canadian agencies that collect statistics on people who self-harm say they tend to be unreliable due to the private nature of the act, studies show that about 400–750 per 100,000 Canadians engage in some form of self-injury to cope with anxiety or emotional pain. The Canadian Mental Health Association explains that people in Canada self-mutilate for the same reason their counterparts in other countries do: "They are not trying to end all feeling; they are trying to feel better. They feel pain on the outside, not the inside."[1]

Self-mutilation is also a growing problem in Europe, particularly Great Britain. According to Steven Levenkron, author of *Cutting: Understanding and Overcoming Self-Mutilation,* one out of every 130 British people is a self-mutilator. The problem is worse among young Brits: Health-care researchers in that country estimate that one in every ten teenagers engages in a destructive, addictive form of self-injury. A British doctor, Dylan Griffiths, speculated that the high rates of self-mutilation in his country were a result of Britain's "must-have culture," explaining that teenagers "feel like failures when they don't get things immediately. Cutting yourself may be one way of relieving that tension and also punishing the people, like your parents, who you may feel are not giving you enough support."[2] But a must-have culture cannot be the only explanation for why people cut. Indeed, one of Great Britain's most famous cutters was the late Princess Diana, who, as royalty, had just about everything a person could ever want. Diana shocked the world when she revealed in a 1995 British Broadcasting Company (BBC) television interview that she had frequently cut her arms and legs as a response to an internal emotional pain. In other situations, Diana recounted attempts to throw herself through a glass cabinet and down a flight of stairs.

While the problem of self-mutilation is growing in wealthy, Western countries, it is simultaneously on the rise in developing nations. Indeed, some studies have revealed that self-mutilation is growing in places such as Sri Lanka, in which one study found significant numbers of young people prone to poisoning themselves as a response to very strict parenting and as a way of coping with bereavement. Self-mutilation has also been documented in Turkey, where researchers of one study found that 21.4 percent of physically abused male and female children exhibited self-destructive behaviors, including head banging, self-biting, self-burning, and self-cutting.

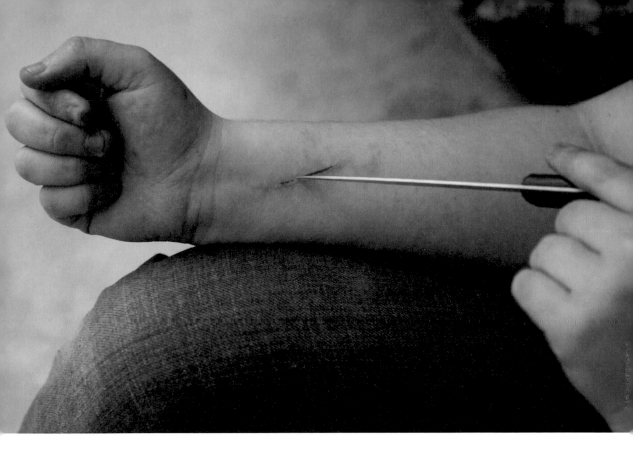

The most astonishing statistics come from Asia. The BBC has reported that Asian women are three times more likely to harm themselves than white women. Such high rates have in some cases been attributed to a history of sexual molestation, but more often women who mutilate themselves do so as the result of being trapped in an abusive or confining marriage. In some Asian cultures, girl children are considered to be less valuable than boys and grow up in a corresponding environment. Married women often play an especially subservient role, both to their husbands and their families, and are not encouraged to be outspoken about their feelings. Sabina Ahmed is one columnist who can attest to the pressures put on Asian women that lead them to self-mutilate. In a column for *Asians in Media*, an online news magazine, she wrote, "You hear women talking about being turned out of their matrimonial home for giving birth to a baby girl; for being blamed if they have been sexually assaulted; of Asian

In order to deal with emotional pain and depression, many people, especially women, will cut themselves to relieve stress.

Celebrities, such as Angelina Jolie, have admitted to cutting or hurting themselves to ease emotional pain.

doctors telling women who have self-harmed themselves to go home and be a good girl—not asking them what the cause of their distress could be."[3]

That self-injury is a problem creeping across the globe has not escaped the attention of health-care providers, mental health experts, school administrators, parents, and teachers in a growing number of countries. The challenges they face in treating sufferers of this disorder, along with the growing prevalence of the problem, are just two of the topics explored in *Writing the Critical Essay: An Opposing Viewpoints Guide: Self-Mutilation*. What drives people to self-mutilate, whether plastic surgery, tattoos, and extreme piercings qualify as self-mutilation, and what role the Internet plays in encouraging or helping people recover from self-mutilation are explored in carefully edited viewpoints. Model essays and thought-provoking writing exercises help readers develop their own opinion and write their own narrative essays on this compelling and disturbing subject.

Notes

1. Quoted in Jane Brody, "The Growing Wave of Teenage Self-Injury," *New York Times*, May 6, 2008.

2. Quoted in Rebecca Traister, "Self-Mutilation on the Rise in Britain," *Salon.com*. November 28, 2005. http://dir.salon.com/story/mwt/broadsheet/2005/11/28/cutting.

3. Sabina Ahmed, "Our Culture Is Driving Women to Harm Themselves," AsiansinMedia.org, October 19, 2007. www.asiansinmedia.org/news/article.php/current-affairs/1764.

Section One: Opposing Viewpoints on Self-Mutilation

Teenagers Mutilate Themselves to Cope with Stress and Depression

Sari Grossman and Sandy Fertman Ryan

In the following essay sixteen-year-old Sari Grossman tells the story of how she struggled with a self-mutilation disorder. Grossman began cutting herself as young as four years old as a way of coping with stress, sadness, and fear. Her problems continued through middle school, where she was routinely teased by classmates. Social problems quickly led to academic ones, and before she knew it Sari was cutting herself to relieve the stress she felt from conflict with her parents, teachers, and class-mates. After much counseling, Sari learned to deal with her emotional stress and depression without resorting to physical pain.

Sari Grossman wrote this essay when she was sixteen years old. She received help from Sandy Fertman Ryan, an author whose articles have been published in *Girls' Life*, where this essay was originally published.

Consider the following questions:

1. How does Sari say she coped with her parents' divorce?
2. What rehab facility did Sari attend in Chicago, and what was her experience there?
3. In what way did classes like art help Sari to stop cutting herself?

Sari Grossman and Sandy Fertman Ryan, "The Silent Scream," *Girls' Life*, vol. 12, August–September 2005, pp. 68–73. Copyright © 2005 Girls Life Acquisition Corp. Reproduced by permission.

Growing up, I'm sure I seemed like any normal kid. In fact, I probably tried harder to fit in because I was an only child. But on the inside, I always felt like I was totally different—and not as worthy—than everyone else.

My parents divorced when I was 4, and that was really traumatic for me. I just didn't know how to deal with all of the fear and sadness I was feeling. Without thinking, I started scratching my arms and legs with my fingernails until I bled and, for some reason, that was always very comforting to me.

"Blood Poured Out"

I already had skin problems, so my parents just thought I needed to see my dermatologist. But when the dermatologist told them I was scratching myself, they took me to my pediatrician for some answers. He suggested that I use a rubber band to snap on my wrist whenever I had the impulse to scratch myself, but it didn't work. My parents sent me to a therapist and, although that didn't stop me from scratching myself when I got scared, it was nice having a place to talk every week. Eventually, I was diagnosed with Attention Deficit Disorder, so I was put on Ritilin, Concerta and sleep medications.

My life became even more stressful when I started sixth grade. I was living with my mom and was moved from a private to a public school. Since I was "the new kid," I was teased every day, so I always came home crying. It was so horrible. Sometimes, my mom would even have to come and get me or my teacher would send me to the nurse's office—which only made matters worse with other kids in my class. My grades plummeted that year and, for the first time in my life, I got three D's.

When my mom saw my report card, she called my dad, and they both yelled at me. I felt totally ganged up on and just couldn't handle it at all. I ran to the bathroom, locked the door and picked frantically at my skin. Then, I noticed a hair clip on the counter. I was so angry and frustrated that I thought, "If I use this to cut myself, I'll feel better—

Most Common Forms of Self-Injurious Behavior

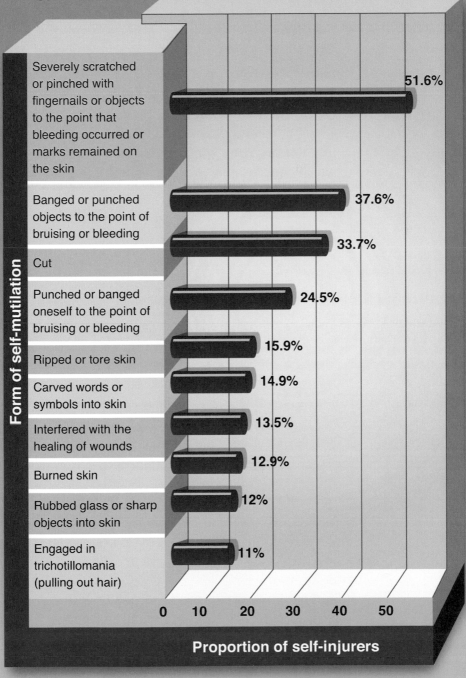

Cutting, scratching, and bruising are the most common forms of self-mutilation.

Form of self-mutilation

- Severely scratched or pinched with fingernails or objects to the point that bleeding occurred or marks remained on the skin — **51.6%**
- Banged or punched objects to the point of bruising or bleeding — **37.6%**
- Cut — **33.7%**
- Punched or banged oneself to the point of bruising or bleeding — **24.5%**
- Ripped or tore skin — **15.9%**
- Carved words or symbols into skin — **14.9%**
- Interfered with the healing of wounds — **13.5%**
- Burned skin — **12.9%**
- Rubbed glass or sharp objects into skin — **12%**
- Engaged in trichotillomania (pulling out hair) — **11%**

0   10   20   30   40   50

Proportion of self-injurers

Taken from: Whitlock J., Eckenrode J., and Silverman D., "Self-Injurious Behaviors in a College Population." *Pediatrics*. 2006;117:1939–1948.

and they'll understand how depressed I am." So I used the clip to cut myself on my arms, and blood poured out.

Cutting to Feel Calm

As odd as it sounds, I suddenly felt completely calm. My mom finally broke into the bathroom with a screwdriver and, when she saw that I was bleeding, she held me and cried. Right away, my parents realized they had been too hard on me and, although they did want me to get better grades, they came to the realization that my problem wasn't about slacking off at school.

After that, I always hid my scar. When anyone notice it, I'd just say my cat scratched me. I think I was embarrassed because I was afraid people would think I was suicidal, which I wasn't. I just wanted to feel relaxed—and that's how I felt when I bled. I continued scratching, but I never cut myself with anything for the rest of that year.

The Razor's Edge

I thought seventh grade would be better than sixth, but it was really tough on me for different reasons. I felt bombarded with every emotion—about friends, school, parents, boys—and it was too much to take. I had a boyfriend who became totally controlling, telling me what to do, what music to listen to and what to wear. Although I eventually dumped him, I was so upset that I began cutting myself again. This time, though, I used a razor blade. I know some kids cut themselves for attention, but I didn't. I cut myself to feel better about my life.

That summer, my friend convinced me to go with her to camp, so I went but hated it! I got really sick and begged the counselors to let me call my parents. At first, they wouldn't let me but then the camp director said if I

Teenagers Mutilate Themselves to Cope with Stress and Depression

According to recent research, 17 to 20 percent of high school and college students are intentionally harming themselves. A large percentage of them never talk about it.

Melinda Alvarado, "Cutting an Addiction," *Fox News*, November 28, 2007.

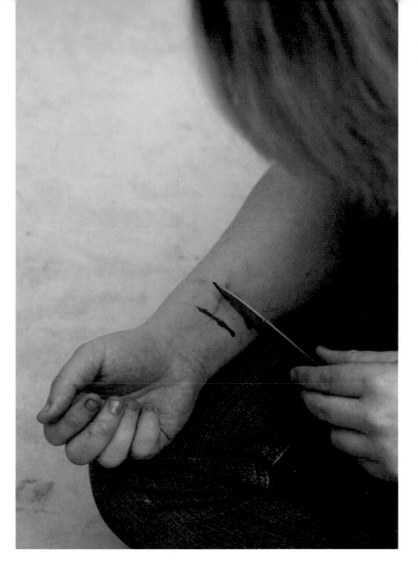

Many teenagers' lives become so stressful that they turn to lacerating themselves to relieve stress.

did this three-hour hike with everyone, he'd let me call home. I did the hike but, afterward, he changed his mind and said I couldn't call. I freaked! I was furious that he had lied to me, and I felt like screaming every foul word at him but couldn't. I grabbed a plastic knife, went off on my own and cut my arms.

A couple of days later, parents were allowed to visit the camp and, when I saw my mom, I told her what had happened. She felt terrible and said, "We're taking you home."

I stayed "clean" until school started, but I was put on higher doses of my medications, plus an anti-depressant. The meds helped but, when the doctor kept increasing

Why People Self-Mutilate

A variety of factors–stress, loneliness, feeling unable to cope–lead people to harm themselves. As a result, they report feeling relieved, in control, and alive.

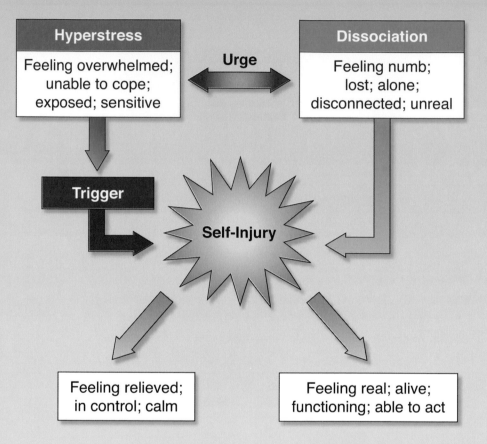

Taken from: LifeSIGNS (Self Injury Guidance and Network Support; www.lifesigns.org.uk).

the dosages, my life spun out of control. I felt like I was crazy, so I used candles to burn my hands, and knives to cut my arms and legs. I felt I had to do something for relief from all the feelings I had building up. Usually, I cut myself after school or before bedtime since it helped me sleep. My mom couldn't help noticing my new scars, and she felt completely frustrated and helpless. I hated myself for hurting her, but I couldn't stop myself. The therapy and medications clearly weren't working.

Desperate Times, Desperate Measures

Everything came to a head in the fall. I was shaking violently in school and thought the world was going to end. It was the worst feeling. I had no idea what was happening to me. Someone dragged me to the nurse's office, and my mom came to get me. We went to my doctor, who immediately cut my dosages.

My mom found me a new therapist but, soon after that, my parents got in this huge fight over my cutting and that threw me over the edge. I pleaded for them to stop, and my dad stormed out. I locked myself in the bathroom and cut myself. My arms and wrists bleeding, and fully clothed, I got in the shower and lay there with the water running over me. My mom broke into the bathroom, crying, and said, "Sari, you need rehab." I totally agreed. Not only was I completely out of control, but I was so angry at myself for hurting my parents when all I wanted to do was hurt myself.

In December, I checked into Self Abuse Finally Ends (SAFE) in Chicago. I was scared, but it started off pretty good because I discovered there were lots of other girls who had the same problems. I realized I wasn't crazy, but then I relapsed by cutting myself with my fingernails. I also got in trouble for jokingly hitting my roommate. I was kicked out of the program after only 15 days, and I felt so ashamed for failing.

My mom was angry at the staff for giving up on me, and she was beyond desperate. My therapist suggested a teen therapy group in Los Angeles with a psychotherapist named Dr. Elaine Leader. I went to weekly meetings at her house and, although I didn't stop cutting right away, it helped me immediately. Everyone there felt like family to me.

Learning to Deal with Emotional Pain

Starting high school was like a whole new beginning. I made new friends and had cool classes, like art, which gave me a way to express myself. I was also the lead

Many teens who attend therapy sessions for self-mutilation find out they are not alone and that many other teens have the same problems.

singer in my own band. I felt freer than I ever had. But by November, my new boyfriend had completely broken my heart. I saw a big knife at home and hacked up my arms, hoping I would feel better. But this time when I bled, it was different. I didn't feel calm. Instead, I thought, "Why am I doing this?!" I was dizzy and felt like vomiting. Suddenly, the cutting thing seemed so stupid. I was disgusted. That was about a year and a half ago, and it was the last time I hurt myself. Looking back, I think I hurt myself to replace emotional pain with physical pain. Somehow, physical pain was easier to deal with.

I've always hidden my scars under long sleeves and pants, but now I accept them as part of me. They are a reminder of what I went through and that I never want to go through it again. They make me proud of how far I've come. Now I know how to deal with things as they come up.

Analyze the essay:

1. This essay differs from the other essays in this section in that it is a first-person narrative, or someone's account of an event in their own words. In what way do first-person narratives differ from other types of essays? What are their strengths? What are their weaknesses? Evaluate how hearing Sari's story in her own words made you feel about her problem.

2. Sari says she turned to self-mutilation because it was easier for her to feel physical pain rather than emotional pain. If Sari was your friend, how would you help her with this problem? What might you say to her? How might you show her that she does not need to cut herself to cope with her emotions?

Girls Are Prone to Self-Mutilation

T. Suzanne Eller

In the following essay T. Suzanne Eller examines how girls, especially middle- and upper-class teenage girls, are prone to cutting or otherwise hurting themselves to deal with emotional pain. Eller spotlights the stories of several girls who have struggled with self-mutilation at some point during their adolescence. By talking to several self-injurers, Eller learns that teenage girls cut themselves to feel like they have control over their lives. She reports that cutting gives them a sense of calm, which is a welcome respite from the stress of their lives. Finally, cutting is a coping method for girls who have trouble communicating their feelings: Instead of telling people they are in pain, they show they are in pain by inflicting it on their bodies. Eller concludes that although self-mutilation is a difficult topic, girls who feel inclined to cut themselves must realize they are in trouble and should work with their parents to get the help they need.

Eller is the author of *Real Issues, Real Teens—What Every Parent Needs to Know*. She speaks to audiences of teenagers and parents and contributes regularly to *Today's Christian Woman*, from which this essay was taken.

Consider the following questions:

1. According to Eller, what constitutes self-mutilating behavior?
2. Who is Brooke Shewmaker, and what is her story, as told by the author?
3. What are endorphins, and what role do they play in self-mutilating behavior, as reported by the author?

T. Suzanne Eller, "Cutting Edge: Why Even Christian Teens Aren't Immune from the Epidemic of Self-Mutilation," *Today's Christian Woman*, vol. 28, January–February 2006, pp. 38–42. Copyright © 2006 Christianity Today, Inc. Reproduced by permission.

She lingered behind the others, waiting to speak to me after my workshop at a Christian parenting conference.

"My daughter's hurting herself," the woman whispered, her eyes brimming with tears. "I don't know what to do."

She'd discovered faded marks on her daughter's arms a few days earlier. When she inquired about the scars, her daughter made an excuse. But later, when the mother passed her daughter's half-opened bedroom door and caught her changing, she spotted fresh cuts running up and down her child's legs. When she confronted her daughter, she was stunned to discover additional self-inflicted cuts to her daughter's torso.

"I've asked myself a hundred times what I did wrong," the woman told me. "My daughter's 15. She's bright. She has friends. I didn't know anyone did this. . . .

Self-Mutilation Affects All Kinds of Girls

This behavior has many names: cutting, self-injury, self-mutilation, self-violence. It includes not only cutting but also scratching, picking scabs, burning, punching, bruising or breaking bones, or pulling out hair. Though death isn't the goal of this deliberate, repetitive harm to one's body, it can cause scarring, infection, and even fatality if a cut goes too deep or an infection isn't treated.

Self-injury crosses economic brackets, education, race, gender, and age. But the majority of those involved are middle- to upper-class adolescent girls. Exact statistics are hard to pinpoint because the behavior often is hidden. But one thing's clear: The growing trend of self-injury isn't confined to teens outside the church. As a youth worker, I've connected with Christian teens for more than 15 years. Until two years ago, self-injury was rarely mentioned. That's changed.

"I Feel So Trapped"

Recently I attended a basketball game with several Christian teens. When a player swished a three-pointer,

One in Six Teens Is a Cutter

Girls are more than twice as likely as boys to cut themselves to deal with stress and depression, but the trend is growing among boys as well.

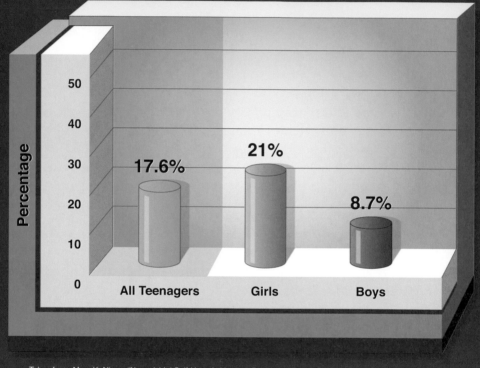

Taken from: Mary K. Nixon, "Nonsuicidal Self-Harm in Youth: A Population-Based Survey," *Canadian Medical Association Journal*, vol. 178, no. 3, January 29, 2008, pp. 306–312.

we jumped to our feet to celebrate, and a girl in front of me threw her hands up in the air. That's when I saw the faded scars that ran down the length of one arm; two small cuts veered across the large vein on her hand. Without thinking, I placed my hand over the cuts, and she jerked down her sleeve.

"How long have you been cutting?" I asked quietly.

She sat next to me, slowly raised her sleeve, and revealed the path of emotional pain marked by razor blades. "I've never told anybody about this," she said. "'I'm only talking to you because you didn't freak out.

The last thing I want is for my Christian friends to think I'm evil or possessed. I love God with all my heart. But I feel so trapped."

A Way to Gain Control

Brooke Shewmaker, a 20-year-old college student I met while conducting research, told me that when she was 16, she hid behind locked doors so her mom wouldn't discover her self-injuring activities. Brooke carved her arms with a razor blade and later moved to her stomach. Brooke called her stomach her "billboard," etching on it feelings

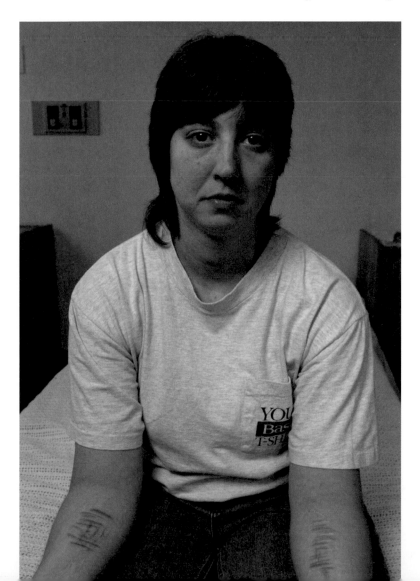

A young woman shows her arms, marred by years of self-mutilation.

she couldn't communicate with anyone else. I had to ask Brooke the question that loomed large in my mind: Why would any teen secretly inflict pain on her body?

"In some ways, it felt like the only control I had at the time," Brooke told me. "I felt rejected. My mother was a counselor but didn't have time to talk to me. My father lived in a different state. Boyfriends failed me, and I didn't know Jesus for whom he was. I wanted something I could control, a sense of power—and cutting gave me that."

According to Lysamena, a former cutter who's been a Christian since age 11, "I know people whose self-injury started because they were so disgusted with themselves, they felt hurting themselves was the only logical thing to do."

Cries for Help

When parents see the wounds on their teen's arms, they often react in fear, shock, and anger. They threaten. They beg. They want it to stop. According to Wendy Lader, Ph.D., founder of S.A.F.E. Alternatives, a residential program for self-injurers, "Two common reactions are either to become furious at the teen and to punish her, or to minimize the behavior as a phase or bid for attention and to ignore it."

But Leslie Vernick, licensed counselor at Christ-Centered Counseling for Individuals and Families, says a teen's really saying, Help, I'm hurting and I don't know how to deal with my pain!

"Endorphins released during cutting often soothe some deeper emotional pain—rejection, depression, self-hatred, or helplessness," Vernick explains. A teen who self-injures finds instant release through the biochemical reaction and correlates cutting with comfort.

Girls Are Prone to Self-Mutilation

"I found my razor blades. I cut my wrist just enough for it to bleed. I couldn't stop crying. I wanted to be able to dig the blade into my arm, but I kept crying. I wanted to die so badly. I wanted to bleed. I was clenching my wrist with my other hand and I could see the blood gushing between my fingers."

Jolene Siana, quoted in Ryan E. Smith, "Scars Relate Stories of Teenage Torment," *Blade* (Toledo), March 12, 2006.

Where Do People Mutilate Themselves?

Self-mutilators typically attack their arms, hands, wrists, and legs.

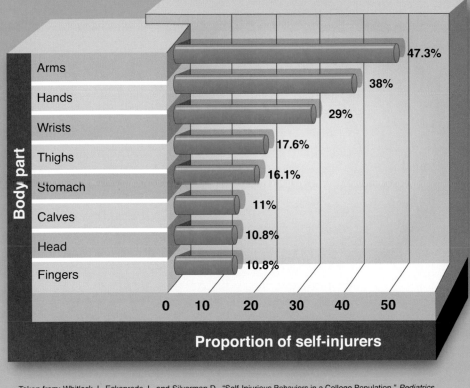

Taken from: Whitlock J., Eckenrode J., and Silverman D., "Self-Injurious Behaviors in a College Population." *Pediatrics*. 2006;117:1939–1948.

Lader describes self-injury as "self-medication." Cutters haven't learned to express their emotions, so the feelings persist. "The teen uses physical pain to communicate something she's unable or unwilling to put into words," explains Vernick. "She needs help to process whatever emotional pain she feels so she'll learn healthy ways of dealing with hurts instead."

The first step for parents is to focus on your teen's deeper emotional needs. "If you discover your child's self-injuring, ask lots of questions. Is this a one-time thing? Is it a pattern? What did your child hope to accomplish by doing this?" Vernick advises. "Check other body parts.

Arms and legs are favorite spots for cutting; if you spot old marks, don't hesitate to get professional help ASAP."

Marissa's Story

A year ago, my friend Channi, a recent divorcee, discovered her youngest daughter, Marissa, was cutting herself.

"This isn't something you share at Bible study," Channi told me. "I was afraid they wouldn't understand, or worse, judge my daughter or me."

Channi and Marissa went to a Christian family counselor. There Channi discovered Marissa was angry and felt abandoned by her father. Marissa suppressed her feelings because the whole family was struggling and she didn't want to be a burden. Cutting became her release.

After several sessions, Marissa began talking openly about her feelings. The counselor also connected Marissa with an older teen who once self-injured but was now free of cutting. They became e-mail friends.

The Path to Recovery

Brianna, the teen I met at the basketball game, has ridden the self-injury roller coaster for more than three years. She started cutting when she was 14. At first, her parents disciplined her, scolded her, and watched her every move. But after three years, they realized the problem wasn't going away. They found a counselor, and Brianna began weekly sessions.

Brianna's recovering, but in the past two months she relapsed twice. Brianna's greatest challenge? She feels alone in her recovery. When she tries to let her parents know she's tempted, they respond with, "That's what the counselor is for."

I talked with Channi recently; and her report was more enthusiastic. "Marissa's still seeing a counselor, who assures me she's doing well, and I believe it. We have an open-door policy in our house, and if any of us is struggling, we pray about it together."

Warning Signs

Without becoming overbearing, Channi watches for warning signs such as long sleeves and pants in hot weather. Channi and Marissa are also aware of triggers—anything that causes a strong desire to cut impulsively. Triggers include music, websites, or blogs (online public diaries) devoted to self-injury. Marissa's computer is in full view of everyone at home and has filtering software.

Together Channi and Marissa rid the house of shaving razors (Marissa bought hair-removal cream) and any ordinary item that seemed harmless to Channi but tempted her daughter (such as a ruler Marissa kept in her notebook).

Channi let Marissa know how much she was loved, even when she lapsed. If Marissa felt tempted to cut or actually self-injured, despite her shame and guilt, she knew she could go to her mom. Channi learned to react without fear or anger.

Teens with self-mutilation disorders often dress in long-sleeve shirts and pants, even during hot weather.

"If I'd focused on the injury rather than what was going on in Marissa's life, we'd still be struggling," Channi says. . . .

A Squeamish but Important Topic

The timely message for the hurting mom I met at the conference that day—and for other families struggling with self-injury—is this: God isn't afraid of the tough stuff. There is hope, and there are positive steps to take to find healing.

While self-injury can be a squeamish topic, it's an important one.

Analyze the essay:

1. Instead of relying on facts, statistics, or historical examples the way some of the other essays in this section do to make their arguments, this essay focuses on the narrative stories of Brooke, Lysamena, Marissa, and other girls who have suffered from self-mutilation. In what way does hearing the girls' personal stories affect your interest in the topic of self-mutilation? Might there be certain advantages, or drawbacks, to this particular style of essay writing? Explain your answer thoroughly.

2. To discuss how girls are prone to self-mutilation, T. Suzanne Eller quotes from several experts. Make a list of everyone she quotes, including their credentials and the nature of their comments. Then, analyze her sources—are they credible? Are they well qualified to speak on this subject? What support do they lend Eller's points?

Plastic Surgery Is a Form of Self-Mutilation

Sheila Jeffreys

In the following essay Sheila Jeffreys argues that plastic surgery qualifies as a form of self-mutilation. She describes the extreme lengths to which women go to make their bodies more attractive to men. They risk surgical complication, deformity, even cancer in the pursuit of warping their bodies in the name of beauty. Jeffreys argues that most women get plastic surgery because they are depressed and think changing their body will make them and the men who love them—happier. But Jeffreys argues it is a sick culture that encourages self-mutilation in the pursuit of happiness. She concludes that it is only because Western civilization is misogynistic (has a hatred of women) that plastic surgery is not counted by the United Nations as an act of self-mutilation.

Jeffreys is a feminist scholar and activist and a professor of political science at the University of Melbourne. She is the author of *Beauty and Misogyny: Harmful Cultural Practices in the West*.

Consider the following questions:
1. What two events coincided with the advent of cosmetic surgery in the United States, according to Jeffreys?
2. What connection is there between breast implant surgery and depression and suicide, as reported by the author?
3. How has the hipster pants fashion continued to inspire the mutilation of women, in the author's opinion?

Sheila Jeffreys, "Beauty and Misogyny," *Arena Magazine*, August–September 2005, pp. 46–50. Copyright © 2005 Arena Printing and Publications Pty. Ltd. Reproduced by permission.

According to United Nations documents such as the 'Fact Sheet on Harmful Traditional Practices', harmful cultural/traditional practices are understood to be damaging to the health of women and girls, to be performed for men's benefit, to create stereotyped roles for the sexes and to be justified by tradition. . . . [But] western beauty practices from make-up to labiaplasty do fit the criteria and should be included within UN understandings. . . .

Socially Approved Self-Injury

Changing attitudes and practices will not be easy, however, particularly given the normalisation of cosmetic surgery. For example, according to Elizabeth Haiken in her book *Venus Envy*, between 1982 and 1992, the percentage of people in the US who approved of cosmetic surgery increased by 50 percent and the percentage who disapproved decreased by 66 percent. Cosmetic surgery, she says, began at the same time in the US as the phenomenon of beauty pageants and the development of the beauty industry in the 1920s. . . .

Cosmetic surgery, as Haiken points out, was always about putting women into the beauty norms of a sexist and racist society. Women who did not fit American norms had to [be] cut up. Thus by the mid-century, 'Jewish and Italian teenage girls were getting nose jobs as high school graduation presents'.

Breast augmentation, however, is more recent than other types of cosmetic surgery and dates from the early 1960s. This places its origins in the so-called sexual revolution in which men's practice of buying women in prostitution was destigmatised through the ideology of sexual liberalism. The sex industry expanded swiftly in the US through pornography and stripping. Breast augmentation was associated in the beginning with 'topless dancers and Las Vegas showgirls'. The method of enlarging breasts for men's pornographic delight in this early period was silicone injections rather than implants. . . .

Health Risks of Beauty-Driven Manipulation

The effects on the health of victims of this harmful cultural practice were very severe. The silicone 'tended to migrate'. It could turn up in lymph nodes and other parts of the body, or form lumps that would mask the detection of cancer. As Haiken comments: 'At worst, then, silicone injections could result in amputation, and at the very least all recipients were expected to have "pendulous breasts" by the time they were forty'. In 1975 it was reported that 'surgeons suspected that more than twelve thousand women had received silicone injections in Las Vegas alone; more than a hundred women a year were seeking help for conditions ranging from discoloration to gangrene that developed anywhere from one to fourteen years later.'

Silicone implants replaced injections but concerns about the health effects caused the American Food and Drug Administration to impose an almost total ban in April 1992. Women who received implants regularly

Many teens feel the need to have cosmetic surgery in order to fit into society's perception of beauty.

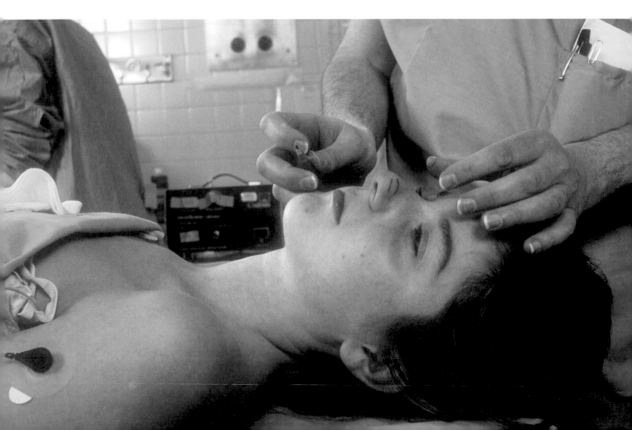

lost sensation in their nipples after the surgery and suffered problems such as encapsulation when scar tissue rendered the breasts hard. Saline implants were favoured where silicone was outlawed. Nonetheless, by 1995, when *Glamour* magazine asked men, 'If it were painless, safe, and free, would you encourage your wife or girlfriend to get breast implants?', 55 per cent said yes. This figure does indicate where the pressure for women to have implants originates.

One impulse that underlies women's pursuit of breast implant surgery may be depression. Several studies have shown that there is an unusually high suicide rate among those who have implants. A 2003 Finnish study found that the rate was three times higher than among the general population. There is controversy as to the reason for this high rate. Some researchers say it indicates that women who have implants are already depressed and have a tendency towards suicide.

The high rate would then suggest that the surgery does not cure the depression. Others say that the suicides may relate to the degree of pain and anxiety women suffer because of the implants. Either way, the suicide rate suggests that breast implants are not positively correlated with women's mental health. . . .

The Mutilation and Death of Lolo Ferrari

[Lolo] Ferrari is a woman who was constructed, and driven to her death, by men's pornographic demand for women with large breasts. Her life story serves as a grave example of the way men's fetish demands can be carved onto the bodies of women, and the effect this can have on women's lives. Ferrari was in the Guinness Book of Records for possessing the biggest breasts in the world. They weighed one-eighth of her body weight. She died in March 2000, apparently of an overdose of prescription drugs. She had made several suicide attempts previously. . . .

The cosmetic surgery operations began in 1990 after her marriage to Eric Vigne. Vigne sketched the results he would like to see for the surgeon and her chest was increased from thirty-seven to forty-one inches, her nose was reduced, her cheekbones accentuated, her lips filled with collagen and her eyes lifted. Her eyebrows were shaved and replaced with tattooed lines. There were more than twenty operations to come over the next four years, with five to six surgeons operating on her. New implants took her chest size to forty-five inches. . . .

Star Lolo Ferrari had over 20 cosmetic and breast augmentation surgeries in four years. Her depression over the ordeal led her to overdose on prescription drugs.

The Mutilation of Models and Actresses

Ferrari's experience may be the most extreme lengths to which breast implant sadism towards women can go, but there are other women following in her wake. The Australian magazine *NW*, which, like other women's gossip sheets, likes to cover the harmful practices carried out on celebrities, dedicated an article in 2001 to photos of women they considered to be seriously inconvenienced by what had been done to their chests. The UK model Jordan had apparently had three 'boob jobs' costing [Australian dollars] AUD$28,350, leaving her frame 'grossly out of proportion' with a size 32FF chest. The magazine helpfully includes a diagram showing how Jordan, on 20cm heels, as she is pictured, has dangerously shifted her centre of gravity. . . .

The US actor, Pamela Anderson, is going along the same path. She had breast implants taking her to a size 34D in 1989, and had them replaced by larger implants taking her to 34DD a few years later. She had the implants removed in 1999. In 2001 she had new implants put in and replaced these with larger ones almost immediately, according to *NW*. All this is despite the fact that she has had the problem of leaking implants.

Midriff Mutilation

The body types featured in sexual entertainment spawn other forms of extreme mutilation of women. The hipster pants fashion, particularly as portrayed by Britney Spears, has led to a surge in lipo-surgery to create Britney-style flat stomachs. *NW* features a woman who undertook the nine-hour operation, costing thousands of dollars, because she was 'so embarrassed by her belly'. The patient, Hilary Coritore, explains: 'I'd just like to feel proud of my figure, but right now I'm so ashamed of my belly—it just hangs there. Britney Spears has an amazing stomach, and I'd give anything to look like that. She wears all those low pants and I just wish I could have a stomach as flat as hers'.

THE SAD IRONY IS THAT THE MORE LIPOSUCTION, IMPLANTS, RESTYLANE AND BOTOX I GET...

THE MORE "AMERICAN" I LOOK.

In the operation, she receives liposuction to her thighs and upper abdomen to help 'show off' the tummy tuck that took place as follows: 'A large 15cm-square slice of Hilary's belly is then cut off and thrown away. The whole area from Hilary's pubic bone up to her navel has been removed'. She received breast implants at the same time to utilise the same incision. Cosmetic surgeons like to give the impression that they perform these mutilations for the sake of the women rather than to exploit women's low self-esteem to line their pockets. . . .

Plastic Surgery Should Count as Mutilation

The forms of mutilation that are socially approved because they make women more sexually attractive to men—cosmetic surgery and some forms of piercing and tattooing—are usually separated out from the wave of self-mutilations of more extreme or unusual varieties involved in body modification. It is not clear to me that they should be, however. The seriously invasive surgery involved in breast implantation, for instance, would be considered savage if it was carried out at a body modification convention. When it is done by surgeons in the name of relieving the supposedly ordinary distress of women about their appearance it can be seen as unremarkable. . . .

In the face of an epidemic in the west of increasingly severe forms of self-mutilation, it may be time to ask how the attacks on the body may be stopped. The fashion, beauty, pornography and medical industries that justify and promote these forms of self-harm are parasitic on the damage male dominant western societies enact on women and girls and vulnerable constituencies of boys and men.

Analyze the essay:

1. Sheila Jeffreys believes plastic surgery should qualify as an act of self-mutilation. What pieces of evidence did she use to support her argument? Do you agree with her? Why or why not?

2. To make her argument that plastic surgery is a form of self-mutilation, Jeffreys uses the stories of Lolo Ferrari, Pamela Anderson, and others. How do these stories serve to support her argument? What pieces of them did you find most interesting or compelling?

Body Art Is a Form of Self-Mutilation

Wendy Lader

In the following essay Wendy Lader argues that body art, such as extreme piercing and tattooing, constitutes a form of self-mutilation. Lader explains that our bodies are like a bulletin board—we use them to communicate messages about ourselves and our feelings. She says that when people get pierced in extreme places, or get tattoos that cover most of their body, they are hiding from their emotions and attempting to cope with fear, isolation, and alienation. In Lader's view, body art is a way for people to gain control over their lives, a way to reclaim themselves from a world in which they feel powerless and alone. She urges people who feel the need to get extreme body art to talk about their feelings and get help, lest they destroy their bodies in the quest to permanently alienate themselves from others.

Wendy Lader is the clinical director of S.A.F.E. Alternatives at Linden Oaks Hospital in Naperville, Illinois, the first structured inpatient program for deliberate self-harm behavior. She has lectured and conducted workshops at numerous professional conferences and has published numerous journal articles regarding self-injury. She is also coauthor of the book *Bodily Harm: The Breakthrough Healing Program for Self-Injurers*.

Consider the following questions:

1. What main similarity is shared by body art and scars from cutters, according to Lader?
2. Name four significant changes in American communities that the author says have resulted in an increased sense of loneliness.
3. In what way does body art create "smoke and mirrors," according to the author?

Wendy Lader, "A Look at the Increase in Body Focused Behaviors," *Paradigm*, Winter 2006. Reproduced by permission.

Throughout the years, I have often been asked whether I believed there is a relationship between self-injury and "body art." When I first started pondering this question, I thought they were very different acts with different meanings and purposes. After all, self-injury is usually a private act inflicted by the individual, whereas body art is often a social act designed to have one fit in or impress a particular peer group. In addition, it is usually performed by someone other than the individual.

However, I came to realize that I was focusing on the differences and missing the more salient similarities. The more thought I gave to this issue the more I have come to believe that there is often only a thin line between those that self-injure and many of those that modify their bodies for the sake of beauty and or art. Is it purely coincidental that people in our society are turning to more permanent avenues of self-expression with their bodies serving as the canvas? . . .

Like Cutting, People Lose Themselves to Body Art

Are these modifications actually visible proclamations of one's true identity? Many people who get tattoos, for example, think long and hard about what they want imprinted on their body to best represent to the world what is important to them. Some people have their whole life story tattooed across their arms, legs and torsos. Self-injurers often state that their scars tell their history as well, even if only to them. Do these various body alterations or designs actually represent one's sense of self, and if so, why are people now experiencing a need to display their internal views of themselves on their bodies? . . .

I postulate that rather than finding one's self through these various body alterations, people are losing themselves. Rather than getting in touch with their feelings, they are numbing. Rather than bringing them closer to their identity, they serve to alienate. Thus youth often spiral out of control as they engage in more and more of these behaviors with less and less sense of self satisfaction.

The Body as a Bulletin Board

The body represents the individual to the outside world. It is how people are recognized from one another. The skin serves as the boundary between "me" and "other"

Many teens turn to tattooing in order to feel better about themselves.

(the rest of the world). It therefore makes sense that the body can represent a personal bulletin board to express to others things about oneself. Is there a fear that if one does not make their body more eye catching then no one will bother to look any further; to spice up the cover, so to speak, in hopes that someone might take an interest in reading the book? Or perhaps the natural body has become so distasteful (or boring) that one needs to find ways to embellish, disguise or disfigure it? And if so, from where does this sense of intense dissatisfaction or boredom originate? . . .

The Relationship Between Body and Alienation

I believe that we are seeing an increase in body-focused behaviors for a myriad of cultural reasons, and that they are not merely a pointless fad. We live in a society that is becoming increasingly disenfranchised. Company loyalty is a thing of the past. Job changes are often accompanied by geographic moves. On top of this, divorce is on the rise as is the phenomena of "blended" families. Kids might not only move across the country with a parent, but also might need to live between two households. Whereas extended families used to live within easy distance of one another, now grandparents, cousins, aunts and uncles can be scattered and live hundreds, if not thousands, of miles from one another. We no longer have a "village" raising our children, nor do adults have the support that closer communities used to provide.

In a world in which kids have more material goods than ever, why do they feel so deprived? Is it possible that the rapid introduction of technology has served to increasingly isolate people from one another? There was a time not so long ago when neighbors sat out on their front porches and knew each other well. The streets would be filled with active kids riding bicycles, playing pick up basketball or just "hanging together" talking about their lives and sharing their dreams. They used to play cards and board games with live people. Now kids go into their homes, bury themselves in their PC's (Personal Computers) and chat or play online games with total faceless strangers. Even when outside amongst other people, they are so absorbed with listening to their I-pods, or cell phone conversations, that they barely notice, much less acknowledge those that pass by. In addition, our society has become more dangerous, and younger people have been indoctrinated with the "stranger danger" philosophy of safety. They are taught not to make eye contact or speak with strangers. They can no longer ride their bikes or walk to school alone. Is it a wonder that our kids often experience themselves as alienated and alone? My friends in AA often remind me, "The mind is a dangerous neighborhood to be walking around in by oneself." . . .

> ## Body Art Constitutes a Form of Self-Mutilation
>
> What was once considered grievous bodily harm has now become the last word in cool. Body mutilation is the decoration of choice for an age which has turned violence into a modish cult. . . . Tattoos expose a terrible hollowness of character [and] reflect a distressing inarticulacy and sense of personal insignificance.
>
> Melanie Phillips, "The Fashion for Self-Mutilation," *Daily Mail* (London), May 24, 2004.

Mutilating the Body as a Way to Cope

Today's youth are being exposed to much more and at earlier ages than they ever were before. Current exposure is a long way from looking at nude pictures in *National Geographic*; children are provided with less structure, limits and opportunity to process what they are exposed to in society. In a world that often seems out of control, the body remains ours to do with what we will. Modifying one's body might therefore provide one with a sense of control, albeit temporary, that might seem too elusive to otherwise attain. I often hear from my self-injuring clients, "It's my body; I can do what I want to it." Changing one's body is often designed to get the attention of others in an effort to decrease one's sense of invisibility, or to gain power over one's enemies by appearing dangerous— such as the vampire look or choosing tattoos designed to intimidate. Samoan fisherman believed that if they could survive their intricate and extensive tattooing process, then they could survive the elements.

Of course most things in life operate on a continuum. Is a butterfly tattoo on one's shoulder, a diet to fit into a pair of size 8 jeans, or a bellybutton piercing indicative of a deeper problem, or merely normal adolescent rebelliousness and a desire to fit in with peers? The behavior is not truly the problem; rather it is the drive and intensity

Changing one's body by applying tattoos is often done to get the attention of others or in an effort to increase self-esteem.

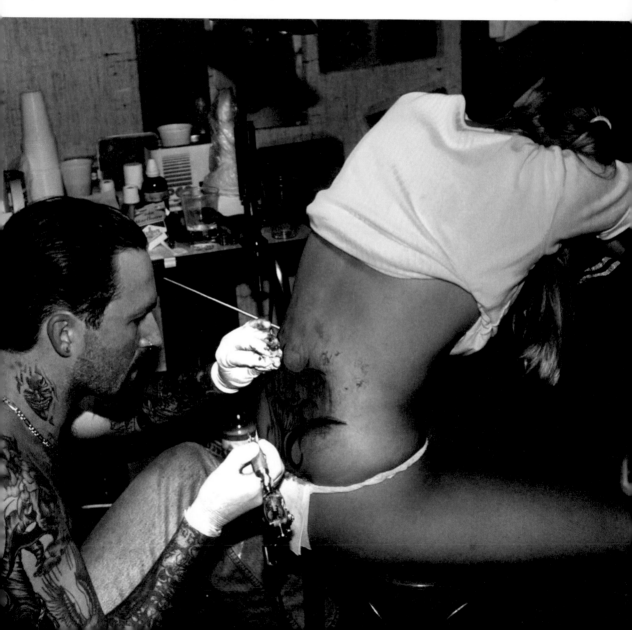

behind the behavior to which clinicians should attend. These body-altering behaviors can serve as a coping strategy, an effort to control the out of control, to distract from the elusive and painful emotional to the tangible and palliative physical.

"Smoke and Mirrors"

I believe that many of these body modifying behaviors are an example of "smoke and mirrors," designed to have clinicians look in one direction, in an effort to keep them from looking in another. It keeps clinicians, as well as the person engaging in the behavior, focused on the physical, rather than the emotional, or stated in another way, focused on the physical at the expense of the emotional. . . .

The less one is able to identify, label and express thoughts and feelings, the more overwhelmed one is likely to be. The less one knows about their internal life and emotional cues, then the more vulnerable one is likely to feel. Moreover, the less one is able to communicate thoughts and feelings to others, the more likely one is to experience oneself as invisible. How can youth communicate these internal experiences to others, to feel connected and understood if they do not have the language of thoughts and feelings? What happens when those internal experiences build to uncomfortably intense, amorphous states? Perhaps, they discharge through action using their bodies, their bulletin boards to "turn up the volume" so that someone might attend and help. . . .

Body Art Buries the Self

In the search for one's identity through modification of the body, one is building a "false self," a mask that at best may make an approximation of the person underneath, but in fact serves to hide and bury the "true self." Many of my clients recite the mantra, "If people really knew me they would not like me." They present a face to the world that is created to defend against the fear of alienation and rejection. However, by failing to identify and accept their true selves, by never taking the risk to allow others to see them with all of their thoughts, feelings and vulnerabilities, they are creating a self-fulfilling prophecy, one that will forever alienate them from both themselves and others.

Analyze the essay:

1. In the essay you just read, Lader uses history and examples to make her argument that body art is a form of self-mutilation. She does not, however, use any quotations to support her point. If you were to rewrite this essay and insert quotations, what authorities might you quote from? Where would you place these quotations to bolster the points Lader makes?

2. Wendy Lader has spent twenty years studying self-mutilation and founded the first inpatient rehabilitation program for people who self-mutilate. Does knowing her background influence your opinion of her argument? In what way?

The Internet Encourages Self-Mutilation

Mary A. Fischer

In the following essay Mary A. Fischer argues that the Internet encourages young people to mutilate themselves. She tells the stories of Joel Evans and Caitlin Scafati, two teens who learned how to hurt themselves by visiting Web sites and chat rooms. While Caitlin turned to cutting Web sites as a way of expressing self-hatred and frustration over her weight, Joel engaged in a dangerous game in which he strangled himself to get a rush. Both teenagers used Web sites and chat rooms to learn, among other things, techniques for hiding their self-mutilation from others. Joel's experimentation ultimately killed him, while Caitlin was left with scars and an eating disorder. Fischer concludes that the Internet is a dangerous tool in the hands of young people who seek to harm themselves.

Fischer is the author of *Stealing Love: Confessions of a Dognapper*. Her articles have appeared in *GQ*, *New York Magazine*, the *Washington Times*, *Rolling Stone*, *People*, *U.S. News & World Report*, and *Reader's Digest*, from which this essay is taken.

Consider the following questions:

1. How many kids does Fischer say accidentally strangle themselves each year?
2. What percent of American teens use the Internet to learn about hard-to-discuss topics, according to the author?
3. Approximately how many self-injurers live in the United States, as reported by Fischer?

Number of Self-Injury Web Sites Is Increasing

More and more self-mutilation Web sites, chat rooms, and message boards are added to the Internet every year.

Year	No. boards	Total membership
1998	1	93
1999	7	949
2000	26	2,831
2001	25	703
2002	28	1,611
2003	19	952
2004	24	806
2005	38	1,698
Total	**168**	**9,643**

Taken from: Janis L. Whitlock, Jane L. Powers, and John Eckenrode, "The Virtual Cutting Edge: The Internet and Adolescent Self-Injury," *Developmental Psychology*, vol. 42, no. 3, 2006, p. 411.

Dangerous Games

Robert and Phyllis Evans considered themselves lucky. They had three wonderful children whom they adored and, after 26 years of marriage, their relationship was still solid. They owned a four-bedroom, two-story house in the woodsy, close-knit town of Mill Valley, California. In their yard, surrounded by wild blackberry bushes, they often saw fawns and bucks with giant antlers.

One evening in November 1999, the Evanses became concerned when they noticed a red, indented mark on their son Joel's neck. It looked like the 14-year-old high school student had pulled his T-shirt tight around his throat. Or maybe someone at school had been rough with him, his father thought.

"What happened to your neck?" his mother asked.

"Oh, it's nothing," Joel said, and went back to playing video games on his computer.

Joel was not a kid you had to worry about, so his parents let it go. He wasn't wild, and he didn't take drugs or drink. He was smart, responsible, even "a little nerdy," by his mother's estimation. He hadn't developed an interest in girls yet; he'd rather spend time on his computer and with his pet rabbit, Fafner. He didn't care that his jeans were too short, or that his straight bangs made him look like a little boy.

His older brother, Daniel, 16, was the risk-taker. He'd recently been sneaking out of the house late at night to meet with friends. Joel, on the other hand, was a more cautious type. Or so his parents thought until March 2000, some months after noticing the mark on his neck, when they came home one afternoon and couldn't find him. Thinking he was playing a favorite game—hiding so he could pop out and surprise them—they continued looking. Phyllis Evans surveyed her son's bedroom a second time and in the dark she saw a shadow by the window. "That's when I found him," she says, her voice trembling. "He had the cord from the mini-blind wrapped around his neck, and he was just hanging there. It was such a nightmare. You just can't believe something like this can happen."

Robert Evans immediately called 911. He cut down his son, laid him on the bed and administered CPR—but it was too late. The coroner ruled the death a suicide, but in part because of Joel's young age, questioned whether it was intentional. None of it made any sense to his parents. This wasn't a troubled kid, or a kid who suffered from depression.

Recently, after seeing TV reports about a disturbing trend popular among teens that goes by various names— pass out, space monkey and the choking game—the Evanses believe they finally know what happened. The red mark on Joel's neck was evidence, they contend, that he had been experimenting with the risky suffocation game in which kids cut off oxygen to their brains momentarily to achieve a euphoric drug-like high. Tragically, it appears that Joel, like some 1,000 youths each year, accidentally strangled himself while playing around with the cord. As for how he learned about the bizarre practice, the Evanses are convinced it was from friends and the Internet.

A Private Pain

Elsewhere in California, in the southern coastal town of Palos Verdes, 14-year-old Caitlin Scafati retreated after dinner most evenings and spent two hours glued to her computer. Nothing unusual about that, her parents thought. That's what kids do these days; they instant message their friends and "chat" for hours at a time. Only Caitlin had other reasons for going online.

A high school freshman, she had trouble adjusting to her school's social cliques and their emphasis on being thin and fashionable. Overweight much of her life and struggling with depression, she felt like an outcast when she became the target of cruel teasing by some of her classmates. "Are you really going to eat that?" a boy once asked Caitlin when he saw her nibbling on a dough-nut. In swim class, a girl took a picture of Caitlin in her swimsuit and posted it in the locker room. "I ripped it up, threw it away and cried most of the night," she says.

In the privacy of her room, Caitlin would log onto the Internet and type in the search words "anorexia" and "cutting." Instantly, dozens of websites appeared that discussed and even promoted the behaviors. Caitlin had turned to both as a way of dealing with her painful emotions and feeling of worthlessness. When she cut her arms and legs, "It made me feel better," Caitlin explains. "I hurt so much inside that this was a way of shifting my pain to the outside."

What Caitlin found online was what she thought she never could in real life—acceptance and understanding from others, many of whom were participating in the same self-destructive behaviors that she was. Instantly available to her were anonymous website contributors who posted comments like: "The thinner I got, the happier I felt," or "I cannot change certain circumstances in my life, but at least I have the power to control what I can do and do not eat." On a cutting website were tips such as, "Cut on a full stomach," and, referring to the direction of the incision, "Always down the road, not across the street."

Unfortunately, experts say, stories of Joel and Caitlin are not uncommon and represent a growing, destructive trend among kids across the United States and around the world. "These practices are spreading like wildfire because of the Internet," says Dr Thomas Andrew, a pediatrician who, in his position as New Hampshire's chief medical examiner, has seen several accidental suffocation deaths among teens in the last few years. According to a 2005 Pew Internet research project, 21 million—or 87 percent of American youth (ranging in age from 12 to 17)—use the Internet as a source of information; 22 percent of them go online to learn more about hard-to-discuss topics like drug use, sexual health or depression.

Psychologists, pediatricians and youth counselors contend that under the radar, hundreds of websites and chat rooms are fueling an explosion of self-destructive practices considered in vogue by a surprising number of kids. They swap techniques about how to injure themselves—and, like Joel and Caitlin, keep it all hidden from their parents.

"Clearly, the Internet is a major tool for good," says Ken Mueller, co-director of CPYU.org, an informational website about youth culture. "But as we're seeing now, it can also lead to great harm. Kids become addicted to these sites, and suddenly behaviors that used to be considered taboo are no longer hidden, which makes them seem more acceptable—even cool."

> ## The Internet Encourages Self-Mutilation
>
> These message boards [devoted to self-mutilation] normalize aberrant behavior. It is also potentially secretive and most self mutilation is clandestine. Teens can either actively or passively participate in chat rooms or message boards. These forums are instructive and teach them how to harm themselves.
>
> Sylvia Gearing, interviewed in *CBS News*, "Cutting Teens," June 11, 2006.

On the Internet, Caitlin found "pro-ana" (short for pro-anorexia) websites that view anorexia nervosa in a positive light—a lifestyle choice rather than a psychological disorder. Suffering from the illness, and losing so much weight that she fainted, the last thing Caitlin needed were tips on how to avoid consuming food—"drink lots and lots of water" or "adopt a dog and feed him your food." Some pro-ana sites provided motivational messages: "Say it now and say it loud: I'm anorexic and I'm proud." Still others bombarded her with color photos of Kate Moss, Calista Flockhart and other thin, beautiful actresses and models to "inspire" her to avoid food.

In May, the first study that examined the impact of eating-disorder websites confirmed their destructive influence. Researchers at Lucile Packard Children's Hospital at Stanford University in Palo Alto, California, found that 40 percent of adolescents who had been hospitalized for eating disorders had spent time on pro-ana websites.

When Caitlin clicked on cutting websites, she found short bios of famous self-injurers, including Princess

Self-destructive teenagers often turn to the Internet where they can find Web sites that promote self-mutilating behavior.

Diana and singer Fiona Apple, which, she says, "made it seem cool and okay." She even discovered sites that gave her tips on how to hide her wounds. On one discussion board, a cutter suggested, "Depending on wear [sic] the cuts are . . . sweatbands will work very well."

"I was amazed to find so many other people with my same problems," Caitlin says. "I felt so isolated, but online I found solidarity from strangers who I felt some connection to."

Though not as common as anorexia—approximately 7 million females and 1 million males suffer from eating disorders—cutting is a growing epidemic among teenage girls. Experts who study self-injury estimate that as many as one out of every 200 teen girls hurt themselves, resulting in 2 million reported cases per year. "Because of the awareness created by these websites," says CPYU. org's Mueller, "cutting has gone from being a way to cope to the hip thing to do."

In fact, studies suggest that there are 3 million self-injurers in the United States. Two million of them cut or burn themselves, while the other million hit, brand, scar, or excessively pierce themselves. "People who cut themselves believe they are horribly flawed in some way," says Wendy Lader, PhD, clinical director of S.A.F.E Alternatives, a referral and treatment program for self-injurers. "It makes them feel strong. They think, I'm not like the rest of you. I'm tough, I can tolerate pain or starvation better than you. But no matter how much they cut or starve themselves, they're not dealing with the real issue—their out-of-control emotions."

Loss and Learning

Robert Evans now believes that for his son Joel, the pass-out game "was something that he thought he could control—something that was secret from us. He didn't have the intent to hurt himself." Asphyxia games— hyperventilating and holding your breath—have been around for decades. One version, autoerotic asphyxia, is used by some older boys and men as a way of intensifying sexual climax. The choking game, done mostly for thrills and often in groups, does not derive from the darker psychological motives behind anorexia and self-injury, but the Internet is fueling more extreme methods.

Google certain keywords and with a few clicks on the right links you'll be connected to a spirited discussion about the choking game. One teen calls it "overrated," while another provides directions about how to play it, including the recommendation: "Have your friend or 'spotter' use his inner wrist to apply pressure to the jugular vein NOT THE WINDPIPE!!!"

"It's about pushing the envelope farther to have an extreme experience," says pediatrician Thomas Andrew, who points to popular television programs like *Fear Factor* to further explain the growing popularity of the choking trend. "We're living in an 'I dare you' culture." Andrew says that kids are adding ropes, belts and plastic bags to the game. "And many are playing alone, which is so dangerous. They don't think of where it can lead. Death is not on their radar screen."

For several years, Yahoo and AOL have been shutting down self-injury sites on their servers. But this kind of information is still available in online chat rooms, which are much harder to police. And short of violating the First Amendment's guaranteed right to free speech, there is frankly no way to eliminate these sites altogether.

What parents need to do, say child-care professionals, is to pay more attention. "There are usually signs, some very obvious, to watch out for," says Lynn Grefe, CEO of the National Eating Disorders Association. Excessive exercise regimens and developing rituals around eating are anorexia tip-offs. A rash of cuts on the body are signs of self-injury. Bloodshot eyes, dizziness and red marks on a child's neck are indications of the choking game.

In 1998, when Caitlin Scafati was 15, she finally decided to talk to her parents about her cutting habits. They

helped her to begin getting the counseling she needed. Now 23, recovered from her disorders and hoping to become a social worker, Caitlin says she had to scar her body and lose an unhealthy amount of weight before she recognized the danger of the sites she was visiting. She has never accessed them again.

Last April, Joel Evans would have turned 20. It was around that time that his father, Robert, having learned more about the choking game, felt a sense of relief. He could in some way finally understand how his son's death came about.

Studies show that in the United States there are over three million self-injurers, two million of which cut or burn themselves.

"We initially had so many questions," says Phyllis Evans, "and doubts." The memory of finding her son that March night will never leave her. But, she says, "five years later, your heart heals a little. The pain is a little less intense."

Analyze the essay:

1. In this essay the author mentions that pro-self-harm Web sites are hard to completely eliminate because they are protected by the First Amendment's right to free speech. What do you think? Should Web sites that feature potentially dangerous content be protected by free speech? Why or why not?

2. Mary A. Fischer concludes that the Internet is more dangerous than helpful for teens who are prone to engage in self-mutilation. How do you think the author of the following essay, Janis Whitlock, would respond to this argument?

The Internet Can Help Some People Recover from Self-Mutilation

Janis Whitlock, Wendy Lader, and
Karen Conterio

In the following essay Janis Whitlock, Wendy Lader, and
Karen Conterio argue that the Internet can help people
who struggle with self-mutilation. A main reason people
self-mutilate, they say, is because they feel isolated and
lonely and are unable to express their emotional pain
to their friends or family. The authors contend that the
Internet allows them to find other people who struggle
with similar issues. Many self-injurers are comforted by
relating to people who know what they are going through,
and online self-mutilation communities, chat rooms, and
message boards allow them this outlet. Furthermore,
most of these sites are run by moderators who put warn-
ings up about sensitive content that might be damaging to
users. Although the Internet has the potential to worsen
self-injurious behavior in some people, the authors conclude that it provides a useful communicative outlet for
most users.

Whitlock is a research scientist in the Family Life
Development Center at Cornell University. She is also the
director of the Cornell Research Program on Self-Injurious
Behavior in Adolescents and Young Adults. Lader and
Conterio are the cofounders of the S.A.F.E. Alternatives
Program.

Consider the following questions:

1. How many active self-injury-focused message boards existed in 2005? In 2006?
2. What does "triggering" mean, in the context of the essay?
3. What percent of respondents said that online self-injury discussion groups had a positive effect on their behavior? What percent said they had a negative effect?

The Internet affords information gathering and social interaction previously unknown to humankind. Individuals can log on to the Internet, from anywhere at any time with privacy and anonymity, and quickly locate vast amounts of information. They can also rapidly locate communities of individuals with shared interests or behaviors. For individuals with interest in or history of self-injury, this capacity makes possible what was previously impossible: rapid identification of others with shared history, experience, and practices. For many, virtual self-injury communities are a gift, an opportunity to reach out of the loneliness and isolation that so often characterizes the practice. For others, however, it poses a risk to recovery. . . .

Availability of Self-Injury Information and Communities

Like many closeted or stigmatized behaviors, such as anorexia, self-injury communities and outlets flourish on the Web. In 2005, we documented over 400 active self-injury-focused message boards; there were well over 500 a year later. A simple query on the Google search engine using terms such as *self-injury*, *self-mutilation*, or *self-inflicted violence*, results in over a million hits. Although it is impossible to verify that all of these are links specific to what we know as self-injury, a brief perusal suggests that many of them are.

Linked blog communities, such as myspace.com or xanga.com provide another means through which individuals seek and share self-injury information and experiences. In a more recent Internet innovation, YouTube. com allows individuals to post videos complete with music and narrative for others to view, comment on, rate, and bookmark. Direct exchange with the video creator is common and often emotionally charged. The site currently features hundreds of self-injury-dedicated videos. The vast majority of these are personal narratives set to music and a cascading set of self-injury related images. . . .

Internet Exchange and the Moderator

Studies show that once online, those engaged in Internet exchange do what people often do offline: exchange support, share personal stories, and voice opinions. In a study

Web sites like MySpace attract individuals who seek and share self-injury experiences.

of self-injury message boards, informal support and discussion of proximal life events that trigger self-injury were the most common types of exchange, followed by casual and sometimes personal information related to the addictive qualities of their practice, their fears relating to disclosure, experiences with psychotherapy, how they self-injure, and other related health concerns.

In most Internet modalities, users are entirely free to observe and post whatever they choose. In Web-based blog communities, such as myspace.com, xanga.com, and facebook.com, anyone can sign up for an account and post content. However, they may not be allowed to post indiscriminately on the sites of other subscribers because posting privileges on each individual blog are dictated by the account holder. YouTube uses a similar format with video creators and is able to control what is and is not posted on their site. Message boards utilize a slightly different format and often vary considerably by degree of moderation.

Moderation level refers to the degree to which posters are actively monitored for potentially damaging content (such as sharing techniques for self-injury) and is typically accomplished by one or more individuals, often the board architects, who judge suitability of posting content. On strongly moderated self-injury message board sites, posting of language or images known or believed to trigger self-injury behavior is actively prohibited. Less-moderated sites will sometimes flag such content as "triggering," so participants can decide whether or not to access the thread. Low-moderated sites lack such oversight and tolerate a wide range of narrative or graphic posts. In these venues, both posters and observers must decide what content is and is not appropriate for their particular needs and vulnerabilities. This can be difficult—particularly for individuals who lack developed capacities to self-regulate, such as young adolescents and individuals particularly vulnerable to images, stories, or sounds which evoke desires to self-injure.

Self-Injury Web Site Content

Self-injury Web sites are most often used for support, but some users are negatively affected by them and visit them to further their addiction to self-harm.

Category	No. of category occurrences	% Posts examined (N = 3,219)*
Informal provision of support for others	913	28.3
Motivation/triggers	629	19.5
Concealment issues	292	9.1
Addiction elements	288	8.9
Formal help seeking, treatment	220	7.1
Requesting, sharing techniques	200	6.2
Links to other mental health conditions	153	4.7
References to popular culture	137	4.2
Interpretation of other's perceptions	85	2.6
Perceptions of self	70	2.1
Venting or apologizing behavior	61	2.9
Uncategorized	277	8.6

*Individual posts could be assigned multiple codes; total percentages will not equal 100%.

Taken from: Janis L. Whitlock, Jane L. Powers, and John Eckenrode, "The Virtual Cutting Edge: The Internet and Adolescent Self-Injury," *Developmental Psychology*, vol. 42, no. 3, 2006, p. 411.

The skills of moderators vary as well. On some self-injury boards, moderators are trained mental health professionals capable of offering feedback and insight as a part of the public exchange. Most often, however, moderators are board architects with little or no training in mental health. Because many self-injury message boards are created by individuals with direct experience, the ability to recognize triggering posts is high. The ability to help posters explore their motivations, however, tends to be far less developed. Some boards and moderators can be actively characterized as pro-self-injury, similar to those documented in reviews of anorexia Web sites. The

Teens may use the Internet to seek out others who can understand their self-destructive behavior.

fact that message boards wax and wane in their activity level and lifespan makes it difficult to identify the most helpful boards. . . .

The Internet holds particular appeal for individuals who self-injure because the assurance of online anonymity is typically comforting to individuals struggling with shame, isolation, and distress. Insecure attachments in early childhood may play a role in the development of self-injury as well as difficulty developing subsequent attachments. Despite the often secretive and hidden nature of the act, however, individuals often report wishing that someone would recognize and understand the intensity of emotional pain that underlies the behavior.

The Internet seems to be especially salient for adolescents and young adults because healthy social and emotional development hinges on their ability to establish meaningful relationships, to find acceptance and belonging in social groups, and to establish interpersonal intimacy. To many, the Internet may become a surrogate friend and/or family where users are able to seek out those who provide not only support, but normalcy as well. Indeed, in a self-report study of whether self-injury discussion groups alleviate or exacerbate self-injurious behavior, 37% indicated that it had a positive effect on their behavior through support of their efforts to cease self-injury and/or through an enhancement of self-acceptance. Only a minority (7%) indicated that they believe the group led to an increase in self-injury.

Such a subjectively positive experience of participation is tempered by the possibility that ongoing and active participation in Internet communities may effectively substitute for the real effort required to develop positive coping and healthy relationships. Unlike face-to-face relationships, which often require work to maintain, Internet relationships are easily disposable; if one friend disappoints, another friend is a mere click away. Because online exchange can fill-in where offline exchange fails, virtual interaction may provide the sense, illusory or real, that core developmental needs for community, intimacy, and honesty are met—at least for awhile. . . .

Such sensitivity may make the Internet a sensory-safe haven for some who practice self-injury. The paradoxical capacity to be instantaneously connected with many others while simultaneously shielded from multiple sensory inputs can appeal to those with heightened emotional sensitivities in real-life exchange. And yet, the ability to effectively interpret and integrate information received from the senses employed in real-life exchange is a critical part of developing healthy coping mechanisms. . . .

The Internet is an inescapable and powerful tool. For those who practice self-injury behaviors, it may be a means of expressing suppressed feelings and of connecting with others like themselves. Because self-expression and healthy connection are critical components of recovery, the Internet may have a productive and effective place in treatment.

Analyze the essay:

1. Whitlock, Lader, and Conterio used research data, logical reasoning, and statistics to make their argument about the Internet's effect on self-injurers. Make a list of all pieces of evidence they used and then say which piece you found most persuasive.

2. In this essay the authors suggest that the Internet can provide a place of comfort and healing for people who self-mutilate. What do you think? Can the Internet provide a constructive forum for people who struggle with self-mutilation, or is it more likely to put more people at risk by encouraging them to do it? Explain your reasoning.

Section Two:
Model Essays
and Writing
Exercises

The Five-Paragraph Essay

An *essay* is a short piece of writing that discusses or analyzes one topic. The five-paragraph essay is a form commonly used in school assignments and tests. Every five-paragraph essay begins with an *introduction*, ends with a *conclusion*, and features three *supporting paragraphs* in the middle.

The Thesis Statement. The introduction includes the essay's thesis statement. The thesis statement presents the argument or point the author is trying to make about the topic. The essays in this book all have different thesis statements because they are making different arguments about cutting and self-mutilation.

The thesis statement should clearly tell the reader what the essay will be about. A focused thesis statement helps determine what will be in the essay; the subsequent paragraphs are spent developing and supporting its argument.

The Introduction. In addition to presenting the thesis statement, a well-written introductory paragraph captures the attention of the reader and explains why the topic being explored is important. It may provide the reader with background information on the subject matter or feature an anecdote that illustrates a point relevant to the topic. It could also present startling information that clarifies the point of the essay or put forth a contradictory position that the essay will refute. Further techniques for writing an introduction are found later in this section.

The Supporting Paragraphs. The introduction is then followed by three (or more) supporting paragraphs. These are the main body of the essay. Each paragraph presents and develops a *subtopic* that supports the essay's thesis statement. Each subtopic is spearheaded by a *topic sentence* and supported by its own facts, details, and examples. The writer can use various kinds of supporting material and details to back up the topic of each supporting paragraph. These may include statistics, quotations from people with special knowledge or expertise, historic facts, and anecdotes. A rule of writing is that specific and concrete examples are more convincing than vague, general, or unsupported assertions.

The Conclusion. The conclusion is the paragraph that closes the essay. Its function is to summarize or reiterate the main idea of the essay. It may recall an idea from the introduction or briefly examine the larger implications of the thesis. Because the conclusion is also the last chance a writer has to make an impression on the reader, it is important that it not simply repeat what has been presented elsewhere in the essay but close it in a clear, final, and memorable way.

Although the order of the essay's component paragraphs is important, they do not have to be written in the order presented here. Some writers like to decide on a thesis and write the introduction paragraph first. Other writers like to focus first on the body of the essay, and write the introduction and conclusion later.

Pitfalls to Avoid

When writing essays about controversial issues such as self-mutilation, it is important to remember that disputes over the material are common precisely because there are many different perspectives. Remember to state your arguments in careful and measured terms. Evaluate your topic fairly—avoid overstating negative qualities of one perspective or understating positive qualities of another. Use examples, facts, and details to support any assertions you make.

The Narrative Essay

Narrative writing is writing that tells a story or describes an event. Stories are something most people are familiar with since childhood. When you describe what you did on your summer vacation, you are telling a story. Newspaper reporters write stories of yesterday's events. Novelists write fictional stories about imagined events.

Stories are often found in essays meant to persuade. The previous section of this book provided you with examples of essays about cutting and other forms of self-mutilation. Most are persuasive essays that attempt to convince the reader to support specific arguments about issues regarding self-mutilation. In addition to making arguments, the authors of these essays also tell stories in which self-mutilation plays a part. They were using narrative writing to do this.

Components of Narrative Writing

All stories contain basic components of *character, setting*, and *plot*. These components answer four basic questions—who, when, where, and what—that readers need to make sense of the story being told.

Characters answer the question of whom the story is about. In a personal narrative using the first-person perspective ("I watched my friend descend into a dark place of depression and self-harm"), the characters are the writer herself and the friend whom she witnesses struggling with self-injury. But writers can also tell the story of other people or characters ("Dr. Thomas founded the self-injury clinic after overcoming a personal struggle with self-mutilation") without being part of the story themselves.

The *setting* answers the questions of when and where the story takes place. The more details given about characters and setting, the more the reader learns about them and the author's views toward them. Mary A. Fischer's description of the Evans's house in Viewpoint 5 provides a good example of vividly describing the setting in which the story takes place. She describes a peaceful, middle-class, suburban house as the unlikely setting of a boy who accidentally kills himself while playing a self-injury game.

The *plot* answers the question of what happens to the characters. It often involves conflict or obstacles that a story's character confronts and must somehow resolve. An example: Julie Brown knows her friend has been cutting herself. Julie must choose between keeping her friend's secret or telling her friend's parents. By keeping her friend's secret she allows her friend to continue to hurt herself. By telling the parents, she risks betraying and angering her friend. How Julie chooses to handle the situation will affect the outcome of the story.

Some people distinguish narrative essays from stories in that narrative essays have a point—that is, in addition to telling a story, the author wants to impress upon the reader a general observation, argument, or insight. In other words, narrative essays also answer "why" questions: Why did these particular events happen to the character? Why is this story worth retelling? Why is it important? The story's point is the essay's thesis. For example, Viewpoint 5 uses the story of Joel Evans to argue that the Internet encourages young people to engage in self-mutilating behavior.

Using Narrative Writing in Persuasive Essays

Narrative writing can be used in persuasive essays in several different ways. Stories can be used in the introductory paragraph(s) to grab the reader's attention and to introduce the thesis. Stories can comprise all or part of the middle paragraphs that are used to support the thesis. They may even be used in concluding paragraphs as a way to restate and reinforce the essay's general point. Narrative essays may focus on one particular story, such as Viewpoint 1, written by Sari Grossman. Or, like Viewpoint 2 which spotlights the stories of Brooke, Lysamena, Marissa, and other girls, narrative essays may draw upon multiple stories to make their point.

A narrative story can also be used as one of several arguments or supporting points. Or, a narrative can take up an entire essay. Some stories are used as just one of several pieces of evidence that an author offers to make a point. In this type of essay, the author usually writes a formal conclusion that ties together for the reader the connection between the story and the point of the essay. In other narrative essays, the story discussed is so powerful that by the time the reader reaches the end of the narrative, the author's main point is clear, and they need not offer a formal conclusion.

In the following section you will read some model essays on self-mutilation that use narrative writing. You will also do exercises that will help you write your own narrative essays.

What Drives America's Teens to Hurt Themselves?

| Editor's Notes | As you read in Preface A, narrative writing has several uses. Writers |

often incorporate the narrative technique into another type of essay, such as a persuasive essay or a cause-effect essay. They may also choose to use narrative only in portions of their essay. Instead of focusing their whole essay on a single story, they may use several different stories together.

This is the structure of the following model essay: It uses pieces of narration to discuss the experience of people who have self-mutilated to cope with anxiety, depression, and emotional pain. As you read, pay attention to the essay's components and how they are organized. Also note that all sources are cited using Modern Language Association (MLA) style*. For more information on how to cite your sources see Appendix C. In addition, consider the following:

1. How does the introduction engage the reader's attention?
2. How is narration used in the essay?
3. What purpose do the essay's quotes serve?
4. Would the essay be as effective if it contained only general arguments, and the stories of Sari Grossman, Brooke Shewmaker, and Caitlin Scafati were not included?

Refers to thesis and topic sentences

Refers to supporting details

Paragraph 1

Across America, teenagers are increasingly engaging in an upsetting and gruesome trend: cutting, bruising, burning, or otherwise hurting themselves to deal with

* Editor's note: In applying MLA style guidelines in this book, the following simplifications have been made: Parenthetical text citations are confined to direct quotations only; electronic source documentation in the Works Cited list omits date of access, page ranges, and some detailed facts of publication.

emotional pain. For outsiders, this behavior can be very difficult to understand. There are many reasons young people self-mutilate, but three main ones come up time and time again when self-injurers tell their stories. Hearing the reasons why young people are driven to mutilate themselves in their own words is a powerful way for outsiders to understand this deeply troubling behavior.

This is the essay's thesis statement: It tells the reader what the essay is about.

Paragraph 2

One reason many self-injurers hurt themselves is to cope with extreme anger. This could be anger over being abused or abandoned by a parent or close relative, anger over the way they are treated at school, or another type of anger. One teen who reports self-mutilating to cope with her intense feelings of anger goes by the name Jane X, to protect her identity. "I cut myself, burn myself, pull out my hair," said Jane. "[When] I get angry and get frustrated, I will pull cups of my own hair. I have tried to break my own bones. It is really embarrassing to admit, I have bruised myself" (qtd. in Alvarado). Unexpressed anger is one of the most common causes of self-mutilation. Self-injurers report feeling soothed, calm, and peaceful after they cut or otherwise hurt themselves.

This is the topic sentence of Paragraph 2. It explores a different facet of the essay's thesis than the other paragraphs do.

The author quotes someone who has personally experienced the problem being discussed. This kind of quote makes an essay more interesting and powerful.

Paragraph 3

Another explanation young people give for mutilating themselves is that they seek a sense of control over their lives. This was the explanation Brooke Shewmaker gave when asked why, as a teenager, she began cutting her arms and stomach with a razor blade. Shewmaker's mother was preoccupied with her job; her father lived in another state. She felt continuously rejected by boys and faced other challenges that gave her a spiraling, out-of-control feeling. For Brooke, cutting was "the only control I had at the time. . . . I wanted something I could control, a sense of power—and cutting gave me that" (qtd. in Eller, 39).

This is the topic sentence of Paragraph 3. It tells what piece of the argument this paragraph will focus on.

Shewmaker's story is paraphrased from Viewpoint 2 in this book.

Paragraph 4

Increasingly, self-injury is paired with another problem, such as a body-image issue or eating disorder. This was Caitlin Scafati's experience—she began cutting herself after being ridiculed by schoolmates about her weight. After enduring cruel teasing and pranks at school, Scafati lost an unhealthy amount of weight and began cutting her arms and legs as a way of channeling her feelings of humiliation and worthlessness. Says Scafati, "I hurt so much inside that this was a way of shifting my pain to the outside" (qtd. in Fischer). Scafati is not alone in having to battle the double demons of self-injury and an eating disorder: According to the Renfrew Center, a reputable eating disorders clinic, 44 percent of their patients admitted to cutting, bruising, or burning themselves. Furthermore, 9 percent of these people reported self-harming at least once a day.

This quote was taken from Viewpoint 5. Learn how to integrate powerful and useful quotes into your writing.

This is a *supporting detail.* This information directly supports this paragraph's topic sentence, helping to prove it true.

Paragraph 5

Feeling angry, out of control, or coping with an eating disorder are three of the most common reasons why young people self-mutilate, but there are many more. Other teens have reported hurting themselves to deal with extreme anxiety, depression, or to come to terms with a past of sexual or other abuse. No matter the reason, any teenager who engages in self-injury needs professional help and the love and support of those around them.

The focus of each paragraph is reviewed in the conclusion.

Note how the essay's conclusion wraps up the topic in a final, poignant way.

Works Cited

Alvarado, Melinda. "Cutting an Addiction." *Fox News* 28 Nov. 2007.

Eller, Suzanne T. "Cutting Edge: Why Even Christian Teens Aren't Immune from the Epidemic of Self-Mutilation." *Today's Christian Woman* Jan–Feb. 2006: 38–42.

Fischer, Mary A. "Thrills That Kill." *Reader's Digest* Feb. 2006.

Exercise 1A: Create an Outline from an Existing Essay

It often helps to create an outline of the five-paragraph essay before you write it. The outline can help you organize the information, arguments, and evidence you have gathered during your research.

For this exercise, create an outline that could have been used to write Model Essay One: "What Drives America's Teens to Hurt Themselves?" This "reverse engineering" exercise is meant to help familiarize you with how outlines can help classify and arrange information.

To do this you will need to

1. articulate the essay's thesis,
2. pinpoint important pieces of evidence,
3. flag quotes that supported the essay's ideas, and
4. identify key points that supported the argument.

Part of the outline has already been started to give you an idea of the assignment.

Outline

I. Paragraph One
Write the essay's thesis:

II. Paragraph Two
Topic: Self-injurers hurt themselves to cope with extreme anger.
   Supporting Detail i. Quote from Jane X describing how she hurts herself when she gets angry.
   Supporting Detail ii. The point about how angry self-injurers feel after hurting themselves.

III. Paragraph Three
Topic:
   i.

   ii. Quote from Brooke Shewmaker describing how feeling out of control causes her to self-mutilate.

IV. Paragraph Four
Topic:

    i.

    ii. Statistic from the Renfrew Center linking self-mutilation and eating disorders.

V. Paragraph Five
    i. Write the essay's conclusion:

Exercise 1B: Create an Outline for Your Own Essay

The first model essay expresses a particular point of view about self-mutilation. For this exercise, your assignment is to find supporting ideas, choose specific and concrete details, create an outline, and ultimately write a five-paragraph essay making a different point about self-mutilation. Your goal is to use narrative techniques to write your essay.

Part 1: Write a thesis statement
The following thesis statement would be appropriate for a narrative essay exploring the link between anxiety and self-mutilation:

> *Everyone feels stressed now and then, but people who self-mutilate suffer from a severe disorder that prevents them from coping normally with stress and anxiety.*

Or, see the sample essay topics suggested in Appendix D for more ideas.

Part II: Brainstorm pieces of supporting evidence
Using information found in this book and from your own research, write down three arguments or pieces of evidence that support the thesis statement you selected.

Then, for each of these three arguments, write down facts, examples, and details that support it. These could be:

- statistical information
- personal memories and anecdotes
- quotes from experts, peers, or family members
- observations of people's actions and behaviors
- specific and concrete details

Supporting pieces of evidence for the above sample thesis statement are found in this book and include:

- Account of Sari Grossman in Viewpoint 1 about how her inability to cope with anxiety led her to cut herself.
- Statistic presented in Viewpoint 6 that 37 percent of self-injurers polled said that the Internet had a "positive effect on their behavior." This could be used to argue that people who self-mutilate because they feel extraordinarily anxious or stressed might benefit from commiserating with other self-injurers online.

Part III: Place the information from Part I in outline form

Part IV: Write the arguments or supporting statements in paragraph form

By now you have three arguments that support the essay's thesis statement, as well as supporting material. Use the outline to write out your three supporting arguments in paragraph form. Be sure each paragraph has a topic sentence that states the paragraph's thesis clearly and broadly. Then, add supporting sentences that express the facts, quotes, details, and examples that support the paragraph's argument. The paragraph may also have a concluding or summary sentence.

Self-Injurers Can Find Support Online

Editor's Notes The following narrative essay differs slightly from the first model essay. Although it is still a five-paragraph essay, it focuses on one story instead of using small pieces of several different stories. Also, instead of just one supporting paragraph, the story takes up most of the essay.

The essay tells the story of Claire, a self-injurer who finds support on the Internet. The characters, setting, and plot are recounted in more detail than they would be in a simple anecdote in order to better engage the reader in the story. In this way the author relies on the power of the story itself to make the essay's point that the Internet can help some self-injurers feel less isolated and lonely and ultimately lead them to treatment.

The notes in the margins provide questions that will help you analyze how this essay is organized and written.

■ Refers to thesis and topic sentences

■ Refers to supporting details

Paragraph 1

Pennsylvania judge J. Stewart Dalzell once described the Internet as "a never-ending worldwide conversation." Indeed, the Internet allows people to communicate no matter where they live, the time of day, and regardless of their budget. People needn't even know each another to arrange lodging in another country; to sell a used couch; or to swap recipes. This facet of the Internet is extremely powerful and useful for people who are suffering from a disorder such as self-mutilation and have no one in their offline world to turn to: This is why self-injurers such as Arizona teenager Claire Mitchell are increasingly turning to the Internet to find support for their problem.

What is the essay's thesis statement?

How did you recognize it?

Paragraph 2

Claire began cutting herself at the age of eleven to cope with her parents' nasty and prolonged divorce. In addi-

Paragraph 2 develops the main character's identity. What kinds of details do you learn about Claire?

This statistic, taken from the visual accompanying Viewpoint 2, supports the paragraph's topic. Get in the habit of supporting the points you make with relevant facts and statistics.

This paragraph describes the story's pivotal event—the act of Claire getting a laptop and using it to find support online.

This is an event that serves to drive the story forward.

What is the topic sentence of Paragraph 4?

tion to feeling like a pawn used by her parents to hurt each other, Claire was unpopular at school. She was often picked last when students paired up for projects and teams and had few classmates she could actually call friends. To deal with her feelings of loneliness and isolation, Claire began cutting herself on her stomach and wrists, parts of the body which a 2006 study found that, respectively, 16.1 percent and 29 percent of all self-mutilators attack. Claire hid her problem with long sleeves and shirts, but her parents were too caught up in their own lives, and probably wouldn't have noticed anyway.

Paragraph 3

When she was fourteen, Claire was given a laptop as a Christmas gift from her father. Claire was excited about the present until she realized her father had only given it to her to spite her mother, who had requested that Claire not receive any presents from him. So depressed over the fight the laptop had sparked, Claire left it unopened on her desk for two weeks, and every look she gave it sent her running to the bathroom, searching for her razor blade. But finally Claire did open it, and she used it to research the subject she was most interested in: self-injury. What she found was dozens upon dozens of sites, chat rooms, and message boards filled with people just like her! A 2005 study documented four hundred active self-injury-focused message boards that year; by 2006 there were more than five hundred. The content of many of these sites is geared toward providing support for self-injurers and also frequently about seeking treatment for and venting about the condition. Claire began reading the messages posted by others and chatting with online users about the feelings that caused her to cut herself.

Paragraph 4

Claire became a regular member of one particular message board and posted to it every time she felt like cutting. As she connected with other self-injurers, Claire became living proof of what researchers at Cornell University found about how online message boards affect self-injurers: "The Internet may become a surrogate friend and/or family where users are able to seek out those who provide not only support, but normalcy as well" (Whitlock et al., 1138). Over time, Claire learned to express her feelings to her online friends instead of bottling them up inside of her. She found herself cutting less and less, and her urge to hurt herself slowly turned into an urge to express herself to others. As a result, Claire would probably count herself among the 37 percent of self-injurers who reported to Whitlock that online self-injury chat rooms and message boards have a positive effect on their behavior in terms of providing them with "support of their efforts to cease self-injury" (Whitlock et al., 1138). By the time she was fifteen, Claire felt strong enough to discuss her problem with her mother, who was able to usher her into a treatment program that helped her end her cutting behavior for good.

This quote was taken from Viewpoint 6 in Section 1. Practice supporting your essays with authoritative quotes.

Paragraph 4 describes the events, actions, and consequences that stem from the pivotal event.

Paragraph 5

Not every site on the Internet can help self-injurers find the strength and support to combat their problem. In fact, a lot of sites encourage self-mutilators to harm themselves further by teaching them tricks and tips and glorifying this very serious and dangerous problem. But some sites hold excellent potential for giving self-injurers the community they lack in their offline life. The online world should, therefore, be considered a useful ally in the fight against self-mutilation.

How does the conclusion return to ideas discussed in the beginning of the essay?

Works Cited

Dalzell, J. Opinion in *ALA v. Department of Justice*, 929 F. Supp. 824. E.D. Pa. 1996.

Whitlock, Janis, et al. "The Internet and Self-Injury: What Psychotherapists Should Know." *Journal of Clinical Psychology* 20 Nov. 2007: 1135–47.

Exercise 2A: Identifying and Organizing Components of the Narrative Essay

As you read in Preface B of this section, narrative essays contain certain elements, including *characters*, *setting*, and *plot*. This exercise will help you identify these elements and place them in an organized structure of paragraphs.

For this exercise you will isolate and identify the components of a narrative essay. Viewpoint 1 (the story of Sari Grossman) and Viewpoint 5 (the story of Joel Evans) from Section I of this book are good sources to practice on, as is *Under the Knife: When the Quest for Perfection Becomes Self-Mutilation*, the next model essay you will read. You may also, if you choose, use experiences from your own life or those of your friends. Part of the exercise is filled out for you using the narrative elements from *Self-Injurers Can Find Support Online*.

Part A: Isolate and write down story elements

Setting

The setting of a story is the time and place the story happens. Such information helps orient the reader. Does the story take place in the distant or recent past? Does it take place in a typical American community or exotic locale?

Model Essay Two	Story Taken from This Volume	Other Story
Arizona Claire Mitchell's house Present day, sometime around 2005–2006		

Character

Who is the story about? If it has more than one character, how are they related? At what stage of life are they?

What are their aspirations and hopes? What makes them distinctive and interesting to the reader?

Model Essay Two	Story Taken from This Volume	Other Story
Claire Mitchell Girl in her early teens Cuts herself to cope with feelings of isolation stemming from her parents' divorce Has no one to talk to about it because she is unpopular at school		

Pivotal Event

Most stories contain at least one single, discrete event on which the narrative hinges. It can be a turning point that changes lives or a specific time when a character confronts a challenge, comes to a flash of understanding, or resolves a conflict.

Model Essay Two	Story Taken from This Volume	Other Story
Claire receives a laptop computer as a gift from her father.		

Events/Actions Leading Up to the Pivotal Event

What are the events that happen to the characters? What are the actions the characters take? These elements are usually told in chronological order in a way that advances the action—that is, each event proceeds naturally and logically from the preceding one.

Model Essay Two	Story Taken from This Volume	Other Story
Because the computer sparked more fighting between her parents, Claire resents it and its presence encourages her to cut herself. But then she starts using it to communicate with other self-injurers in online chat rooms, and their support helps her find strength.		

Events/Actions That Stem from Pivotal Event

What events/actions are the results of the pivotal event in the story? How were the lives of the characters of the stories changed?

Model Essay Two	Story Taken from This Volume	Other Story
Claire slowly replaces her urge to cut with an urge to communicate. She works up the courage to tell her mother about her problem, who helps her get the treatment she needs to stop cutting completely.		

Point/Moral

What is the reason for telling the story? Stories generally have a lesson or purpose that is ultimately clear to the reader, whether the point is made explicitly or implied. Stories could serve as specific examples of a general social problem. They could be teaching tools describing behavior and actions that the reader should either avoid or emulate.

Model Essay Two	Story Taken from This Volume	Other Story
Story is an example of the way in which the Internet can help self-injurers find support among each other and stop self-mutilating.		

Part B: Writing down narrative elements in paragraph form

Since stories vary greatly, telling them can be approached in many ways. One possible way of organizing the story elements you have structured is as follows:

Paragraph 1: Tell the reader the setting of the story and introduce the characters. Provide descriptive details of both.

Paragraph 2: Introduce the plot—what happens in the story. Tell the events in chronological order, with each event advancing the action.

Paragraph 3: Describe the pivotal event in detail and its immediate aftermath.

Paragraph 4: Tell the short-term and/or long-term ramifications of the pivotal event. This paragraph could also include the point or moral of the story.

Paragraph 5: Conclude the story in a memorable and interesting way.

Exercise 2B: Examining Introductions and Conclusions

Most essays feature introductory and concluding paragraphs that are used to frame the main ideas being presented. Along with presenting the essay's thesis statement, well-written introductions should grab the attention of the reader and make clear why the topic being explored is important. The conclusion reiterates the essay's thesis and is also the last chance for the writer to make an impression on the reader. Strong introductions and conclusions can greatly enhance an essay's effect on an audience.

The Introduction

Several techniques can be used to craft an introductory paragraph. An essay can start with:

- an anecdote: a brief story that illustrates a point relevant to the topic.
- startling information: facts or statistics that elucidate the point of the essay.
- setting up and knocking down a position: a position or claim believed by proponents of one side of a controversy, followed by statements that challenge that claim.
- historical perspective: an example of the way things used to be that leads into a discussion of how or why things work differently now.
- summary information: general introductory information about the topic that feeds into the essay's thesis statement.

Problem One

Reread the introductory paragraphs of the model essays and of the viewpoints in Section I. Identify which of the techniques described above are used in the example essays. How do they grab the attention of the reader? Are their thesis statements clearly presented?

The Conclusion

The conclusion brings the essay to a close by summarizing or returning to its main ideas. Good conclusions, however, go beyond simply repeating these ideas. Strong conclusions explore a topic's broader implications and reiterate why it is important to consider. They may frame the essay by returning to an anecdote featured in the opening paragraph. Or they may close with a quotation or refer to an event in the essay. In opinionated essays, the conclusion can reiterate which side the essay is taking or ask the reader to reconsider a previously held position on the subject.

Problem Two

Reread the concluding paragraphs of the model essays and of the viewpoints in Section I. Which were most effective in driving their arguments home to the reader? What sorts of techniques did they use to do this? Did they appeal emotionally to the reader, or did they bookend an idea or event referenced elsewhere in the essay?

Under the Knife: When the Quest for Perfection Becomes Self-Mutilation

Editor's Notes Essays drawn from memories or personal experiences are called personal narratives. The following essay is this type of narrative. It is not based on research or the retelling of someone else's experiences, such as the other narrative essays you have read in this book. Instead, this essay consists of an autobiographical story that recounts memories of an event that happened to the writer.

The essay differs from the first two model essays in that it is written from the subjective, or first-person ("I"), point of view. It is important that you learn to master the personal narrative, as it is this type of essay that is frequently required by college, university, and other academic admissions boards. Personal narratives also tend to be required of candidates seeking to win scholarships and other contests.

The essay is also different from the previous model essays in that it has more than five paragraphs. Many ideas require more than five paragraphs in order to be adequately developed. Moreover, the ability to write a sustained essay is a valuable skill. Learning how to develop a longer piece of writing gives you the tools you will need to advance academically.

■ Refers to thesis and topic sentences

■ Refers to supporting details

Because this is a personal narrative, it does not have the type of thesis statement a more formal essay should have.

Paragraph 1

On some days, I look at myself in the mirror and worry I look a little puffy, or that my forehead is too big. My eyes are kind of on the small side, too, and if I look closely, I freak myself out that they are slightly different sizes. Overall though, I like how I look. I can't say the same for my best friend Rachel.

Paragraph 2

It started with her nose—Rachel always hated it. It did seem a little too big for her face, and had a bump that I found endearing but she saw as horribly flawed. It's important for a girl to like how she looks, however, and so for her high school graduation, Rachel's parents decided to let her get a nose job. She was ecstatic!

How is foreshadowing used in Paragraphs 2 and 3? Foreshadowing is a technique that hints at what might be in store for the characters.

Paragraph 3

"A chance to be a whole new me before going off to college," she said.

"Totally inappropriate," my mom said when she learned about the gift. "What a terrible lesson to teach a child."

Paragraph 4

I didn't think it was such a big deal, though. After all, is a nose job really all that different from dying your hair, getting a tattoo, or piercing your nose? Sure, plastic surgery is more expensive and takes longer to recover from, but at the time I thought it was no different from any other measure a woman might take to make herself look and feel more attractive. In fact, I was kind of jealous that Rachel's parents saw the value in plastic surgery that my own, *au natural* mother did not.

What do you learn about the characters in these sentences? What kind of people are they?

Paragraph 5

Freshman year of college was a busy, exciting time. Rachel and I both made new friends and learned a lot at our respective colleges. We kept in close touch, though, and spoke at least once a week. Shortly before finals, she mentioned she was considering another procedure—this time, a breast augmentation.

Paragraph 6

"Why do you think you need bigger boobs?" I asked her one night on the phone. "The waif look is so in now, anyway."

Does the dialogue sound natural to you? What details or features enhance it?

"I just think I'll feel more confident. I've got this beautiful nose, I want the rest of my body to be worthy of it, you know?"

Paragraph 7

She got the breast augmentation in January, and when we went to Daytona Beach for spring break in March, I had to admit that she looked fantastic.

"See?!" she said, as we lounged on the beach. "I've never felt better about myself!"

Though different from formal essays, personal narratives can still use topic sentences to organize paragraphs and keep them focused on one main idea, as this one does for Paragraph 8.

Paragraph 8

But Rachel's self-esteem soon floundered again, and it seemed like every time we talked there was another surgery she was either looking into or recovering from. Throughout college, the surgical self-improvement continued. In the middle of sophomore year, she underwent a buttock augmentation procedure in which fat was taken from other areas of her body and added to her rear. Junior year she elected to have otoplasty, or ear surgery. This procedure changed the shape of her ears, which she always complained "stuck out unnaturally." Senior year she decided something was horribly wrong with her chin and underwent a complicated procedure in which a silicone implant was placed underneath her jawbone. By the time we graduated from college, I barely recognized her. She looked like a plastic, creepy version of her original self. Deep down I thought she looked awful, an opinion I kept to myself considering all the trouble she'd gone through to look the way she did.

Paragraph 9

Rachel's interest in plastic surgery and her constant need to improve her appearance seemed like an obsession to me, almost like an addiction. I began to read about people who became obsessed with plastic surgery and would stop at nothing to reinvent themselves over and over and over again.

Paragraph 10

My research led me to suspect Rachel suffered from a condition called Body Dysmorphic Disorder (BDD). According to the Anxiety Disorders Association of America, BDD causes people to be abnormally preoccupied with their appearance and become obsessed with real or perceived physical flaws. The AADA says such people "may even undergo unnecessary plastic surgeries to correct perceived imperfections, never finding satisfaction with the results." It sounded exactly like Rachel.

What have you learned about the characters up to this point? What do you learn about them in this paragraph? Are the characters being developed in a way that makes you care about them?

Paragraph 11

It didn't take long for me to have an occasion to share my findings with her. Just a week after graduation, as we were shoe shopping, Rachel informed me she was going to celebrate graduating from college by treating herself to a cheek augmentation.

Paragraph 12

"Mine are so sallow and limp-looking," she said.

I couldn't believe she had found yet another part of her body to hate. "You've got to be kidding me—they're cheeks! What do you expect them to look like?"

"Well it's easy for you to say. You have really nice cheeks. But mine are so. . . ." She trailed off as she frowned at her reflection in a store window.

Paragraph 13

"Stop, just stop." I set down my bags and put my hands on her shoulders. "I think you have a problem. A serious disorder. Something called Body Dysmorphic Disorder. I've been reading about it. It's a condition in which people fixate on their flaws and become addicted to plastic surgery to fix them. I'm really worried about you."

Paragraph 14

She laughed. "You've got to be kidding me! It's nice that you're concerned, but there's *nothing* wrong with me. I think I am beautiful! In fact, I feel *so* beautiful on the inside, I just want my outsides to reflect that."

Paragraph 15

What is the topic sentence of Paragraph 15?

Over the next six years Rachel continued to undergo plastic surgery in her never-ending quest for the perfect body. By the time she was 28 years old, she had undergone 21 cosmetic surgeries. In addition to the first rhinoplasty, ear reshaping, and breast and chin augmentations, she had an additional three nose jobs; one brow lift; repeated Botox injections; cheek implants; veneers placed on her teeth; two lip implants; liposuction on her arms, stomach, hips, thighs, and knees; and more. The total cost of these procedures exceeded $100,000, but the damage done to her physical appearance and mental health was incalculable.

How does this paragraph serve to move the plot forward?

Paragraph 16

Personal narratives are not expected to have a formal conclusion like other essays, but they must still bring the story's ideas to a close.

After losing her job and most of her friends to her plastic surgery obsession, Rachel finally admitted she had a problem. She began intensive rehabilitation for BDD at the age of 29, a course of treatment that included cognitive-behavioral therapy and antidepressants. After five years, she is doing well and hasn't undergone a single procedure, though she admits to me she occasionally wants to. I just smile at her and say, "You know what Rach? I think you look great just the way you are."

Exercise 3A: Practice Writing a Scene with Dialogue

The previous model essay used scene and dialogue to make a point. For this exercise, you will practice creative writing techniques to draft a one- or two-paragraph scene with dialogue. First, take another look at Model Essay Three and examine how dialogue is used.

When writing dialogue, it is important to:

1. Use natural-sounding language.
2. Include a few details showing character gestures and expressions as they speak.
3. Avoid overuse of speaker tags with modifiers, such as "he said stupidly," "she muttered softly," "I shouted angrily," and so on.
4. Indent and create a new paragraph when speakers change.
5. Place quotation marks at the beginning and end of a character's speech.

Scene-Writing Practice

Interview a classmate, friend, or family member. Focus on a specific question about cutting or self-mutilation, such as

- Have you ever known anyone who has cut or otherwise harmed themselves? If so, why did they do it? How did you learn about it?
- What do you think is to blame for the rise in rates of self-mutilation, especially among young people?
- Tell me about the last time you felt anxious, depressed, or emotionally hurt. What triggered your feelings? Where were you? How did you cope with it?
- Do you think that plastic surgery, tattoos, or extreme piercings should qualify as self-mutilation? Why or why not?

Take notes while you interview your subject. Write down what he or she says as well as any details that are provided. Ask probing questions that reveal how the subject felt, what they said, and how they acted. Use your notes to create a brief one- or two-paragraph scene with dialogue.

But I Can't Write That

One aspect of personal narrative writing is that you are revealing to the reader something about yourself. Many people enjoy this part of writing, but others have trouble with sharing their personal stories—especially if they reveal something embarrassing or something that could be used to get them in trouble. In these cases, what are your options?

✔ Talk with your teacher about your concerns. Will this narrative be shared in class? Can the teacher pledge confidentiality?
✔ Change the story from being about yourself to a story about a friend. This will involve writing in the third person rather than the first person.
✔ Change a few identifying details and names to disguise characters and settings.
✔ Pick a different topic or thesis that you do not mind sharing.

Exercise: Write Your Own Narrative Five-Paragraph Essay

Using the information from this book, write your own five-paragraph narrative essay that deals with self-mutilation. You can use the resources in this book for information about self-mutilation and how to structure a narrative essay.

The following steps are suggestions on how to get started.

Step One: Choose your topic.
The first step is to decide what topic to write your narrative essay on. Is there any subject that particularly fascinates you? Is there an issue you strongly support or feel strongly against? Is there a topic you feel personally connected to? Ask yourself such questions before selecting your essay topic. Refer to Appendix D: Sample Essay Topics if you need help selecting a topic.

Step Two: Write down questions and answers about the topic.
Before you begin writing, you will need to think carefully about what ideas your essay will contain. This is a process known as *brainstorming*. Brainstorming involves asking yourself questions and coming up with ideas to discuss in your essay. Possible questions that will help you with the brainstorming process include:

- Why is this topic important?
- Why should people be interested in this topic?
- How can I make this essay interesting to the reader?
- What question am I going to address in this paragraph or essay?
- What facts, ideas, or quotes can I use to support the answer to my question?

Questions especially for narrative essays include:

- Have I chosen a compelling story to examine?
- Does the story support my thesis statement?
- What qualities do my characters have? Are they interesting?

- Does my narrative essay have a clear beginning, middle, and end?
- Does my essay evoke a particular emotion or response from the reader?

Step Three: Gather facts, ideas, and anecdotes related to your topic.

This book contains several places to find information, including the viewpoints and the appendices. In addition, you may want to research the books, articles, and Web sites listed in Section Three or do additional research in your local library. You can also conduct interviews if you know someone who has a compelling story that would fit well in your essay.

Step Four: Develop a workable thesis statement.

Use what you have written down in Steps Two and Three to help you articulate the main point or argument you want to make in your essay. It should be expressed in a clear sentence and make an arguable or supportable point.

Example:

> **Extreme tattoos indicate a person's attempt to disappear beneath a mural of images the same way other self-mutilators attempt to hide their emotions behind cuts, burns, or bruises.**
>
> > This could be the thesis statement of a narrative essay that uses stories about extremely tattooed people to argue that body art is a form of self-mutilation.

Step Five: Write an outline or diagram.
1. Write the thesis statement at the top of the outline.
2. Write roman numerals I, II, and III on the left side of the page with A, B, and C under each numeral.
3. Next to each roman numeral, write down the best ideas you came up with in step three. These should all directly relate to and support the thesis statement.
4. Next to each letter write down information that supports that particular idea.

Step Six: Write the three supporting paragraphs.
Use your outline to write the three supporting paragraphs. Write down the main idea of each paragraph in sentence form. Do the same thing for the supporting points of information. Each sentence should support the paragraph of the topic. Be sure you have relevant and interesting details, facts, and quotes. Use transitions when you move from idea to idea to keep the text fluid and smooth. Sometimes, although not always, paragraphs can include a concluding or summary sentence that restates the paragraph's argument.

Step Seven: Write the introduction and conclusion.
See Exercise 2B for information on writing introductions and conclusions.

Step Eight: Read and rewrite.
As you read, check your essay for the following:

- ✔ Does the essay maintain a consistent tone?
- ✔ Do all paragraphs reinforce your general thesis?
- ✔ Do all paragraphs flow from one to the other? Do you need to add transition words or phrases?
- ✔ Have you quoted from reliable, authoritative, and interesting sources?
- ✔ Is there a sense of progression throughout the essay?
- ✔ Does the essay get bogged down in too much detail or irrelevant material?
- ✔ Does your introduction grab the reader's attention?
- ✔ Does your conclusion reflect on any previously discussed material or give the essay a sense of closure?
- ✔ Are there any spelling or grammatical errors?

Section Three: Supporting Research Material

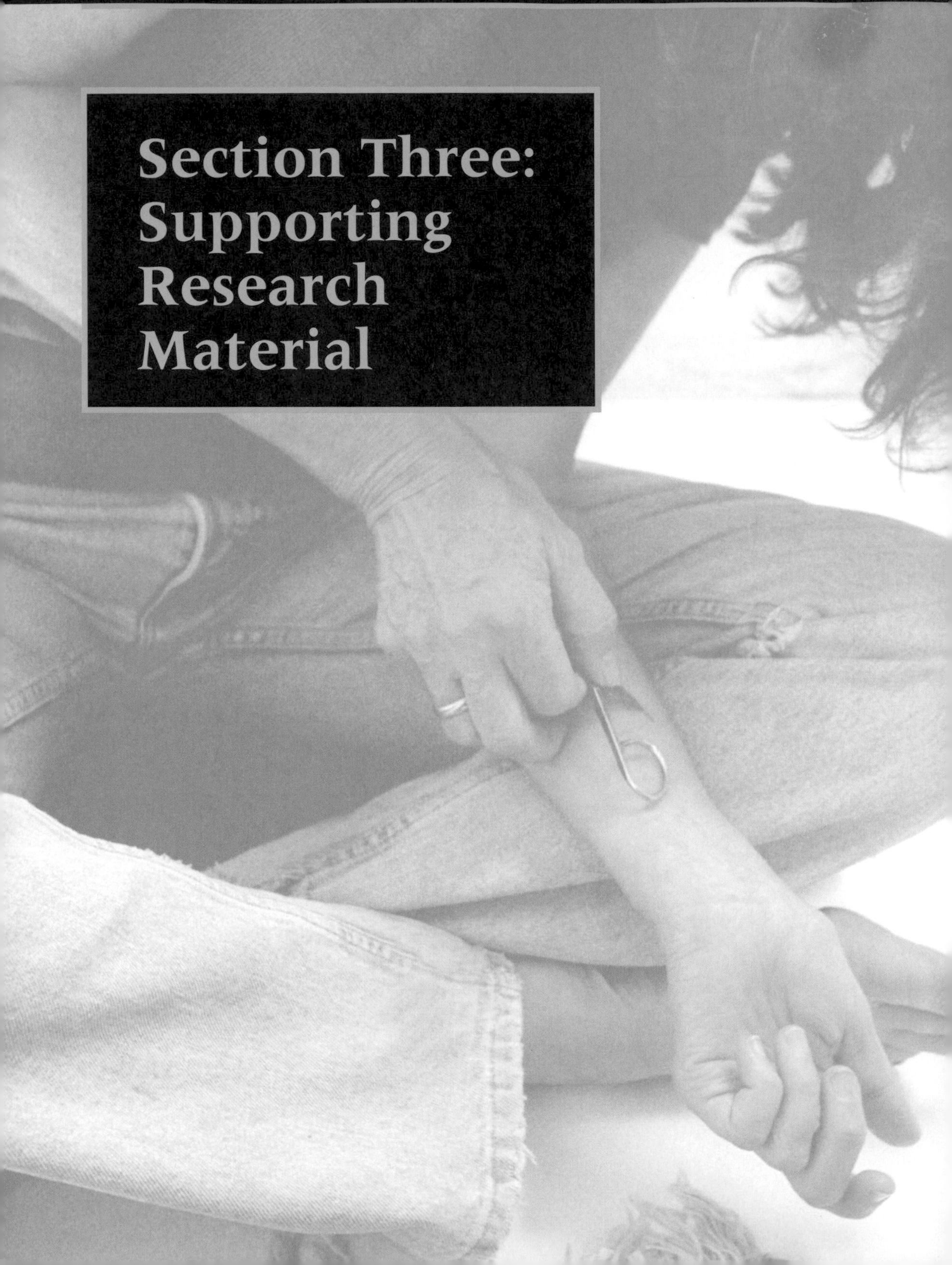

Facts About Self-Mutilation

Editor's Note: These facts can be used in reports or papers to reinforce or add credibility when making important points or claims.

What Is Self-Injury?

According to the organization S.A.F.E. (Self-Abuse Finally Ends), self-injurious behavior is defined as the deliberate, repetitive, impulsive, nonlethal harming of one's self. Self-injury includes:

- cutting;
- scratching;
- picking scabs or interfering with wound healing;
- burning;
- punching self or objects;
- infecting oneself;
- inserting objects in body openings;
- bruising or breaking bones; and
- extreme hair-pulling.

The Scope of Self-Mutilation

A variety of organizations report that an estimated 3 million people in the United States practice self-harm.

According to S.A.F.E.:

- Females are more likely to self-injure than males.
- Self-injurious behavior typically begins at puberty.
- Nearly 50 percent of male and female self-injurers who seek treatment report having been physically and/or sexually abused during childhood.
- As many as 90 percent report that as children they were discouraged from expressing emotions, particularly anger and sadness.

A 2008 study published by the *Canadian Medical Association Journal* found:

- 17.6 percent of teenagers have cut themselves. This is about 1 in every 6 teens.
- Girls are more than twice as likely to cut themselves.
- 21.7 percent of girls report cutting themselves.
- 8.7 percent of boys report cutting themselves.

A 2006 study published in the journal *Pediatrics* found the following about self-injurious behavior:

- 51.6 percent of self-injurers report scratching or pinching themselves so hard that they draw blood or leave marks.
- 37.6 percent report banging or punching objects to bruise or draw blood.
- 33.7 percent report cutting themselves.
- 24.5 percent report punching or banging themselves to bruise or draw blood.
- 15.9 percent report ripping or tearing skin.
- 14.9 percent report carving words or symbols into their skin.
- 13.5 percent report interfering with the healing of wounds.
- 12.9 percent report burning themselves.
- 12 percent report rubbing glass or sharp objects into their skin.
- 11 percent report engaging in trichotillomania, the extreme pulling of hair.

A 2007 Brown University study of 633 high school students found about 46 percent of the students reported some form of self-injury within the previous year.

A 2006 sample of 2,875 American college students found a lifetime prevalence of self-mutilation to be about 17 percent.

A 2006 study published in *Pediatrics* found that self-mutilators typically attack their arms, hands, wrists, and legs:

- 47.3 percent report attacking their arms.
- 38 percent report attacking their hands.
- 29 percent report attacking their wrists.
- 17.6 percent report attacking their thighs.
- 16.1 percent report attacking their stomach.
- 11 percent report attacking their calves.
- 10.8 percent report attacking their head.
- 10.8 percent report attacking their fingers.

According to a 2002 study of self-mutilation in the UK:

- 6.9 percent of 15–16 year old British teens had engaged in at least one act of self-injury in the previous year.
- Only 12.6 percent of self-cutting episodes lead to a hospital visit.
- The peak age for presentation to clinic is 15–24 years for women and 25–34 years for men.
- 30–40 percent of those seeking help after an episode of deliberate self-harm receive a psychiatric diagnosis.
- About 33 percent had received prior psychiatric services.
- Alcohol dependence was diagnosed in 10 percent.
- Schizophrenia and bipolar illnesses were diagnosed in less than 10 percent of self-injurers seeking treatment.

A 2005 study by Britain's Priory, which specializes in treating mental health problems and addictions, found that one in five British girls aged 15–17 has harmed herself.

Reasons People Self-Mutilate

According to the Iowa Psychological Association, self-injurers typically give the following reasons for hurting themselves:

- relief of intolerable stress;
- attempt to regulate unpleasant feeling states;

- poor problem-solving;
- inability to express feelings in words;
- means or attempt to influence others;
- form of self-punishment;
- means of validating self;
- others are doing it; and
- cutting helps me fit in.

According to S.A.F.E.:

- Nearly 50 percent of male and female self-injurers who seek treatment report having been physically and/or sexually abused during childhood.
- As many as 90 percent report that as children they were discouraged from expressing emotions, particularly anger and sadness.

Self-Harm and Other Disorders

According to S.A.F.E.:

Self-harm behavior can be a symptom of several psychiatric illnesses:

- depression/personality disorders (especially Borderline Personality Disorder);
- bipolar disorder (manic-depression);
- mood disorders (especially major depression and anxiety disorders);
- obsessive-compulsive disorder; and
- psychoses such as schizophrenia.

According to the Renfrew Center, an eating disorders clinic:

- 44 percent of their patients admitted to cutting, bruising, or burning themselves.
- 9 percent of these people reported self-harming at least once a day.

Treatment for Self-Mutilation

Common treatment methods for self-mutilation include:

- outpatient therapy;
- partial hospitalization (6–12 hours a day);
- inpatient hospitalization;
- medication, often useful in the management of depression, anxiety, obsessive-compulsive behaviors, and the racing thoughts that may accompany self-injury;
- cognitive-behavioral therapy to help individuals understand and manage their destructive thoughts and behaviors;
- contracts, journals, and behavior logs—useful tools for helping an individual regain self-control;
- interpersonal therapy to help self-injurers gain insight and skills for the development and maintenance of relationships;
- treatment for eating disorders, alcohol/substance abuse, trauma abuse; and
- family therapy.

According to S.A.F.E.:

- People who seek help for self-injury are typically from a middle- to upper-class background, of average to high intelligence, and have low self-esteem.
- Self-injury behavior lasts on average 5–10 years but can be longer without treatment.
- Habitual self-injurers comprise about 1 percent of the population.

Finding and Using Sources of Information

No matter what type of essay you are writing, it is necessary to find information to support your point of view. You can use sources such as books, magazine articles, newspaper articles, and online articles.

Using Books and Articles

You can find books and articles in a library by using the library's computer or cataloging system. If you are not sure how to use these resources, ask a librarian to help you. You can also use a computer to find many magazine articles and other articles written specifically for the Internet.

You are likely to find a lot more information than you can possibly use in your essay, so your first task is to narrow it down to what is likely to be most usable. Look at book and article titles. Look at book chapter titles, and examine the book's index to see if it contains information on the specific topic you want to write about. (For example, if you want to write about whether plastic surgery constitutes a form of self-mutilation and you find a book about cutting, check the chapter titles and index to be sure it contains information about plastic surgery specifically before you bother to check out the book.)

For a five-paragraph essay, you do not need a great deal of supporting information, so quickly try to narrow down your materials to a few good books and magazine or Internet articles. You do not need dozens. You might even find that one or two good books or articles contain all the information you need.

You probably do not have time to read an entire book, so find the chapters or sections that relate to your topic, and skim these. When you find useful information, copy it onto a note card or notebook. You should look for supporting facts, statistics, quotations, and examples.

Using the Internet

When you select your supporting information, it is important that you evaluate its source. This is especially important with information you find on the Internet. Because nearly anyone can put information on the Internet, there is as much bad information as good information. Before using Internet information—or any information—try to determine if the source seems to be reliable. Is the author or Internet site sponsored by a legitimate organization? Is it from a government source? Does the author have any special knowledge or training relating to the topic you are looking up? Does the article give any indication of where its information comes from?

Using Your Supporting Information

When you use supporting information from a book, article, interview, or other source, there are three important things to remember:

1. *Make it clear whether you are using a direct quotation or a paraphrase.* If you copy information directly from your source, you are quoting it. You must put quotation marks around the information, and tell where the information comes from. If you put the information in your own words, you are paraphrasing it.

Here is an example of a using a quotation:

Self-mutilation expert Wendy Lader suggests that people who tattoo themselves extremely are attempting to bury their real self: "In the search for one's identity through modification of the body, one is building a 'false self,' a mask that at best may make an approximation of the person underneath, but in fact serves to hide and bury the 'true self.'" (18)

Here is an example of a brief paraphrase of the same passage:

Self-mutilation expert Wendy Lader suggests that people who tattoo themselves extremely are attempting to bury their real self. She likens their tattoos to a mask that serves to protect or distort a person's true self. She encourages clinicians to dig deeper to find this true self that has been covered over by extreme body art.

2. *Use the formation fairly.* Be careful to use supporting information in the way the author intended it. For example, it is unfair to quote an author as saying, "Cutting is a fad," when he or she intended to say, "Even if cutting is a fad, it is a serious problem that needs professional treatment." This is called taking information out of context. This is using supporting evidence unfairly.

3. *Give credit where credit is due.* Giving credit is known as citing. You must use citations when you use someone else's information, but not every piece of supporting information needs a citation.

   - If the supporting information is general knowledge—that is, it can be found in many sources—you do not have to cite your source.
   - If you directly quote a source, you must cite it.
   - If you paraphrase information from a specific source, you must cite it.

If you do not use citations where you should, you are *plagiarizing*—or stealing—someone else's work.

Citing Your Sources

There are a number of ways to cite your sources. Your teacher will probably want you to do it in one of three ways:

- Informal: As in the example in number 1 above, tell where you got the information as you present it in the text of your essay.
- Informal list: At the end of your essay, place an unnumbered list of all the sources you used. This tells the reader where, in general, your information came from.

- Formal: Use numbered footnotes or endnotes. Footnotes or endnotes are generally placed at the end of an article or essay, although they may be placed elsewhere depending on your teacher's requirements.

Works Cited

Lader, Wendy. "A Look at the Increase in Body Focused Behaviors." *Paradigm* Winter 2006: 14–15, 18.

Using MLA Style to Create a Works Cited List

You will probably need to create a list of works cited for your paper. These include materials that you quoted from, relied heavily on, or consulted to write your paper. There are several different ways to structure these references. The following examples are based on Modern Language Association (MLA) style, one of the major citation styles used by writers.

Book Entries

For most book entries you will need the author's name, the book's title, where it was published, what company published it, and the year it was published. This information is usually found on the inside of the book. Variations on book entries include the following:

A book by a single author:
> Simon, Jonathan. *Governing Through Crime: How the War on Crime Transformed American Democracy and Created a Culture of Fear*. New York: Oxford University Press, 2007.

Two or more books by the same author:
> Mernissi, Fatima. *Beyond the Veil*. San Francisco: Saqi Books, 2003.
> ———. *Fear of the Modern World*. New York: Basic Books, 2002.

A book by two or more authors:
> Esposito, John L., and Dalia Mogahed. *Who Speaks for Islam? What a Billion Muslims Really Think*. Washington, DC: Gallup Press, 2008.

A book with an editor:
> Friedman, Lauri S., ed. *Writing the Critical Essay: Democracy.* Farmington Hills, MI: Greenhaven, 2008.

Periodical and Newspaper Entries

Entries for sources found in periodicals and newspapers are cited a bit differently from books. For one, these sources usually have a title and a publication name. They also may have specific dates and page numbers. Unlike book entries, you do not need to list where newspapers or periodicals are published or what company publishes them.

An article from a periodical:
> Bauer, Henry H. "The Mystery of HIV/AIDS." *Quadrant* July–Aug. 2006: 61–64.

An unsigned article from a periodical:
> "The Chinese Disease? The Rapid Spread of Syphilis in China." *Global Agenda* 14 Jan. 2007.

An article from a newspaper:
> Bradsher, Keith. "A New, Global Oil Quandary: Costly Fuel Means Costly Calories." *New York Times* 19 Jan. 2008: A2.

Internet Sources

To document a source you found online, try to provide as much information on it as possible, including the author's name, the title of the document, date of publication or of last revision, the URL, and your date of access.

A Web source:
> Butts, Jeffrey. "Too Many Youths Facing Adult Justice." Urban Institute. 25 Aug. 2004. < http://www.urban.org/publications/900728.html >. Accessed May 7, 2008.

Your teacher will tell you exactly how information should be cited in your essay. Generally, the very least information needed is the original author's name and the name of the article or other publication.

Be sure you know exactly what information your teacher requires before you start looking for your supporting information so that you know what information to include with your notes.

Sample Essay Topics

Self-Mutilation Is a Serious Problem

The Problem of Self-Mutilation Has Been Exaggerated

Self-Injurers Are Suicidal

Most Self-Injurers Are Not Suicidal

Girls Are Prone to Self-Mutilation

Self-Mutilation Affects Boys as Well as Girls

Body Art Is a Form of Self-Mutilation

Body Art Is Not a Form of Self-Mutilation

Body Art Is a Marker of Cultural Identity

Body Art Is a Sign of Cultural Depravity

Plastic Surgery Is a Form of Self-Mutilation

Plastic Surgery Boosts Self-Esteem

The Media Causes Self-Mutilation

Celebrities Encourage Young People to Self-Mutilate

The Internet Encourages Self-Mutilation

The Internet Can Help Self-Mutilators Recover

Sexual Abuse Causes Self-Mutilation

Depression and Anxiety Cause Self-Mutilation

A Variety of Factors Trigger Self-Mutilation

Web Sites That Promote Self-Mutilation Should Be Censored

Web Sites That Promote Self-Mutilation Should Not Be Censored

Self-Help Strategies Can Reduce Self-Mutilation

Self-Injurers Need Professional Help

Organizations to Contact

American Psychiatric Association (APA)
1000 Wilson Blvd., Ste. 1825, Arlington, VA 22209
(703) 907-7300 • fax: (703) 907-1085 • e-mail: apa@psych.org
Web site: www.psych.org

An organization of psychiatrists dedicated to studying the nature, treatment, and prevention of mental disorders, the APA helps create mental health policies, distributes information about psychiatry, and promotes psychiatric research and education. It publishes the *American Journal of Psychiatry* monthly and a variety of books and newsletters, some of which deal with cutting and other forms of self-mutilation.

American Psychological Association (APA)
750 First St. NE, Washington, DC 20002-4242
(202) 336-5500 • fax: (202) 336-5708
e-mail: public.affairs@apa.org • Web site: www.apa.org

The American Psychological Association is the largest scientific and professional organization representing psychology in the United States and is the world's largest association of psychologists. It publishes numerous books, journals, and videos, several of which are focused on self-injury.

American Self-Harm Information Clearinghouse
521 Temple Pl., Seattle, WA 98122 • (206) 604-8963
e-mail: ashic@selfinjury.org • Web site: http://selfinjury.org

This organization strives to increase public awareness of the phenomenon of self-inflicted violence and the unique challenges faced by self-injurers and the people who care about them. Its Web site debunks myths about self-injury and offers authoritative resources on the subject.

Canadian Mental Health Association (CMHA)

595 Montreal Rd., Ste. 303 Ottawa ON K1K 4L2 Canada
e-mail: info@cmha.ca • Web site: www.cmha.ca

The Canadian Mental Health Association is one of the oldest voluntary organizations in Canada. Its programs are designed to assist people suffering from mental illness find the help needed to cope with crises, regain confidence, and return to their communities, families, and jobs. It publishes books, reports, policy statements, and pamphlets, many of which are focused on self-injury.

CrisisLink

2503 D N. Harrison St. PMB#114, Arlington, VA 22207
(703) 527-6603 • Web site: www.crisislink.org

CrisisLink is a community-based nonprofit organization dedicated to crisis prevention, intervention, and response. In the past thirty-six years, CrisisLink has answered more than half a million crisis calls. Though it primarily serves the Northern Virginia/Maryland/DC region, its Web site has a whole section devoted to cutting and self-harm.

National Institute of Mental Health (NIMH)

6001 Executive Blvd., Rm. 8184, MSC 9663, Bethesda, MD 20892-9663 • (301) 443-4513 • fax (301) 443-4279
e-mail: nimhinfo@nih.gov • Web site: www.nimh.nih.gov

NIMH is the federal agency concerned with mental health research. It plans and conducts a comprehensive program of research relating to the causes, prevention, diagnosis, and treatment of mental illnesses. It produces various informational publications on mental disorders and their treatment, including self-harm.

National Mental Health Association

2001 N. Beauregard St., 12th Flr., Alexandria, VA 22311
(800) 433-5959 • fax: (703) 684-5968
e-mail: nmhainfo@aol.com • Web site: www.nmha.org

The advocacy organization is concerned with combating mental illness and improving mental health. It promotes research into the treatment and prevention of mental illness, monitors the quality of care provided to the mentally ill, and provides educational materials on mental illness and mental health. It publishes the monthly newsletter *The Bell* as well as fact sheets and articles on self-injury.

National Self-Harm Network

PO Box 7264, Nottingham NG1 6WJ, England • e-mail: info@nshn.co.uk • Web site: www.nshn.co.uk

This British organization campaigns for the rights and understanding of self-injurers. It aims to challenge assumptions and common misconceptions about and raise awareness of self-injury.

S.A.F.E. Alternatives (Self-Abuse Finally Ends)

7115 W. North Ave., Ste. 319, Oak Park, IL 60302 (800) 366-8288 • Web site: www.selfinjury.com

This organization boasts a nationally recognized treatment approach for people who self-mutilate. It offers a professional network and educational resource base, which is committed to helping people end self-injurious behavior.

Trichotillomania Learning Center, Inc. (TLC)

207 McPherson St., Ste. H, Santa Cruz, CA 95060-5863 (831) 457-1004 • e-mail: info@trich.org • Web site: www. trich.org

TLC is a national nonprofit organization established to provide information, support, and referral sources regarding the experience and treatment of trichotillomania (compulsive hair pulling). TLC's educational resources are available to people with TTM, their family members and friends, therapeutic professionals, educators, and anyone with an interest in the subject. TLC's mission is to raise public awareness, to maintain a support network and treatment referral base, and to raise funds for research to find a cure for trichotillomania.

Bibliography

Books

D'Onofrio, Amelio A., *Adolescent Self-Injury: A Comprehensive Guide for Counselors and Health Care Professionals*. New York: Springer, 2007.

Esherick, Joan, *The Silent Cry: A Teen's Guide to Escaping Self-Injury and Suicide*. Broomall, PA: Mason Crest, 2005.

Miller, Dusty, *Women Who Hurt Themselves*. New York: Basic Books, 2005.

Nicole, Tara L., *Dancing in the Rain: The Final Cut*. Kent, England: Pneuma Springs, 2006.

Plante, Lori G., *Bleeding to Ease the Pain: Cutting, Self-Injury, and the Adolescent Search for Self*. Westport, CT: Praeger, 2007.

Polak, Monique, *Scarred*. Toronto: James Lorimer, 2007.

Periodicals

Ahmed, Sabina, "Our Culture Is Driving Women to Harm Themselves," AsiansinMedia.org, October 19, 2007. www.asiansinmedia.org/news/article.php/current_affairs/1764.

Alvarado, Melinda, "Cutting an Addition," *Fox News*, November 28, 2007.

Baird, Julia, "Self-Mutilation or Beauty—It's Only a Fine Line," *Sydney Morning Herald* (Sydney, Australia), July 22, 2002.

Baran-Unland, Denise M., "Self-Injury Finds a Voice," *Herald News* (Joliet, IL), August 30, 2007.

Booth, Stephanie, "Cutting Clubs," *Teen People*, April 2004.

Brody, Jane, "The Growing Wave of Teenage Self-Injury," *New York Times*, May 6, 2008.

Cengel, Katya, "Addicted to Pain," *Courier Journal*, September 28, 2003.

Davis, Jeanie Lerche, "Cutting: Parents' Nightmare: Form of Self-Injury Draws More Attention and Is Growing," *CBS News.com*, August 16, 2005. www.cbsnews.com/stories/2005/08/16/health/webmd/main781173.shtml.

Gary, Sydney, "Wounds, Scars and the Visibility of Self-Injury," *Brown University Child and Adolescent Behavior Letter*, vol. 20, no. 3, March 2004.

Katie, S., "Self-Harm: Can Someone Please Help," *Indian Life*, January/February 2007.

Kirn, Timothy F., "Kids and Self-Injury: 'Pain Makes Them Feel Alive,'" *Pediatric News*, April 2007.

Kluger, Jeffrey, "The Cruelest Cut," *Time*, May 9, 2005.

Lader, Wendy, "Treating Self Injuring Clients," *Counselor Magazine*, September 30, 2006. www.counselormagazine.com/content/view/342/1.

Lambert, Aurélie, and Anton F. de Man, "Alexithymia, Depression, and Self-Mutilation in Adolescent Girls," *North American Journal of Psychology*, vol. 9, no. 3, 2007.

Liotine, Julie, "Not Just Skin Deep," *Chicago Parent*, May 25, 2007.

Lundquist, Ben, "Self-Abuse Among Teens Shouldn't Be Ignored," *Naperville Daily Herald*, July 22, 2005.

Moyer, Michael, and Kaye Welch Nelson, "Investigating and Understanding Self-Mutilation: The Student Voice," *Professional School Counseling*, vol. 11, no. 1, October 2007.

Nelson, Karen, "Deliberate Self-Injury: Prevalence and Treatment Strategies," *Iowa Psychologist*, May 2007. www.selfinjury.com/pdf/Iowa%20Psychological%20Association%20Newsletter.May07.pdf.

Phillips, Melanie, "The Fashion for Self-Mutilation," *Daily Mail* (London), May 24, 2004.

Smith, Ryan E., "Scars Relate Stories of Teenage Torment," *Blade* (Toledo), March 12, 2006.

Swartz, Tracy, "Hooked on Suspension," *Chicago Tribune Redeye*, November 9, 2007.

Teen Vogue, "In the Cut," June 2004, p. 144.

Tharp, Bridget, "Stress, Anxiety Lead to Cutting," *Rockford Register Star,* October 21, 2007.

Traister, Rebecca, "Self-Mutilation on the Rise in Britain," *Salon.com,* November 28, 2005. http://dir.salon.com/ story/mwt/broadsheet/2005/11/28/cutting.

Zimmerman, Janet, "A Way to Deal," *Press-Enterprise* (Riverside, CA), August 1, 2004.

Web Sites

Focus Adolescent Services: Self-Injury (www.focusas.com/ Selfinjury.html). This Web site, supported by the Focus Adolescent Services, contains a wealth of information on self-injury in adolescents and features a special section on what parents can do about the problem.

Lysamena Project on Self-Injury (www.self-injury.org). A Christian site devoted to the problem of self-mutilation.

Secret Shame (Self-Injury Information and Support) (www.palace.net/ ~ llama/psych/injury.html). This Web site offers information and anonymous support to people who self-mutilate and to their friends and loved ones.

Self-Injury and Related Issues (SIARI) (ww.siari.co.uk). A valuable online resource, based in the United Kingdom, for self-injurers and anyone interested in the complex phenomenon of self-injury.

Self-Mutilators Anonymous (http://selfmutilatorsanony mous.org). Self-Mutilators Anonymous is a fellowship of men and women who share their experiences and struggles with cutting and self-injury. The organization's goal is that members may solve their common problem and help others to recover from physical self-mutilation.

Index

Picture Credits

About the Editor

Lauri S. Friedman earned her bachelor's degree in religion and political science from Vassar College in Poughkeepsie, New York. Her studies there focused on political Islam. Friedman has worked as a nonfiction writer, a newspaper journalist, and an editor for more than eight years. She has extensive experience in both academic and professional settings.

Friedman is the founder of LSF Editorial, a writing and editing business in San Diego. She has edited and authored numerous publications for Greenhaven Press on controversial social issues such as oil, the Internet, the Middle East, democracy, pandemics, and obesity. Every book in the *Writing the Critical Essay* series has been under her direction or editorship, and she has personally written more than eighteen titles in the series. She was instrumental in the creation of the series, and played a critical role in its conception and development.